JOSIAH MCELHENY

Josiah McElheny

Dave Hickey
Jennifer R. Gross

Isabella Stewart Gardner Museum

Boston, Massachusetts

This book is published in conjunction with the exhibition
"Josiah McElheny," January 22–April 25, 1999, at the
Isabella Stewart Gardner Museum, Boston.

Published by the Trustees of the Isabella Stewart Gardner
Museum, Two Palace Road, Boston, Massachusetts 02115.

Photographs are courtesy of AC Project Room, New York, New
York; Donald Young Gallery, Chicago, Illinois; and the Art
Institute of Chicago, Chicago, Illinois. Page 7: *Church Service for
Poor People* (detail), 1998. Courtesy the Artist; AC Project Room,
New York, New York; and Donald Young Gallery, Chicago,
Illinois.

Designer: Ruth Abrahams
Typefaces: Fournier and Gill Sans
Printer: Meridian Printing, East Greenwich, Rhode Island
Photographers: Ron Amstutz, pages 25, 27, 29, 37; Claire Garoutte,
pages 7, 23, 31, 33, 39, 41, 43, 45, 47, 49, 55, 56; Peter Muscato,
pages 51, 53; Stephen White, page 35.

Distributed by University Press of New England,
Hanover and London

LIBRARY OF CONGRESS CATALOGING-IN-PUBLICATION DATA
Hickey, Dave, 1940-
    Josiah McElheny / Dave Hickey, Jennifer R. Gross.
       p. cm.
    Published in conjunction with an exhibition held at the
Isabella Stewart Gardner Museum, Boston, Mass., Jan. 22–
Apr. 25, 1999.
    Includes bibliographical references.
    ISBN 0-9648475-9-0
    1. McElheny, Josiah, 1966–   —Exhibitions. 2. Glass
art—United States—History—20th century—Exhibitions.
I. McElheny, Josiah, 1966– . II. Gross, Jennifer R.
III. Isabella Stewart Gardner Museum. IV. Title.
NK5198.M44A4 1999   98-43221
748.2913–dc21   CIP

*Sponsorship of artist programming is made possible by the Barbara Lee Program
Fund. Major support for "Eye of the Beholder" programs has been provided by
The Pew Charitable Trusts, the Stratford Foundation, The Boston Foundation,
GTE, and the Clipper Ship Foundation.*

*A portion of the Museum's program operating funds for this fiscal year has also
been provided through grants from the Institute of Museum and Library Services, a
Federal agency, and the Massachusetts Cultural Council, a state agency that also
receives support from the National Endowment for the Arts.*

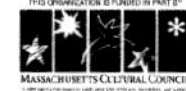

Contents

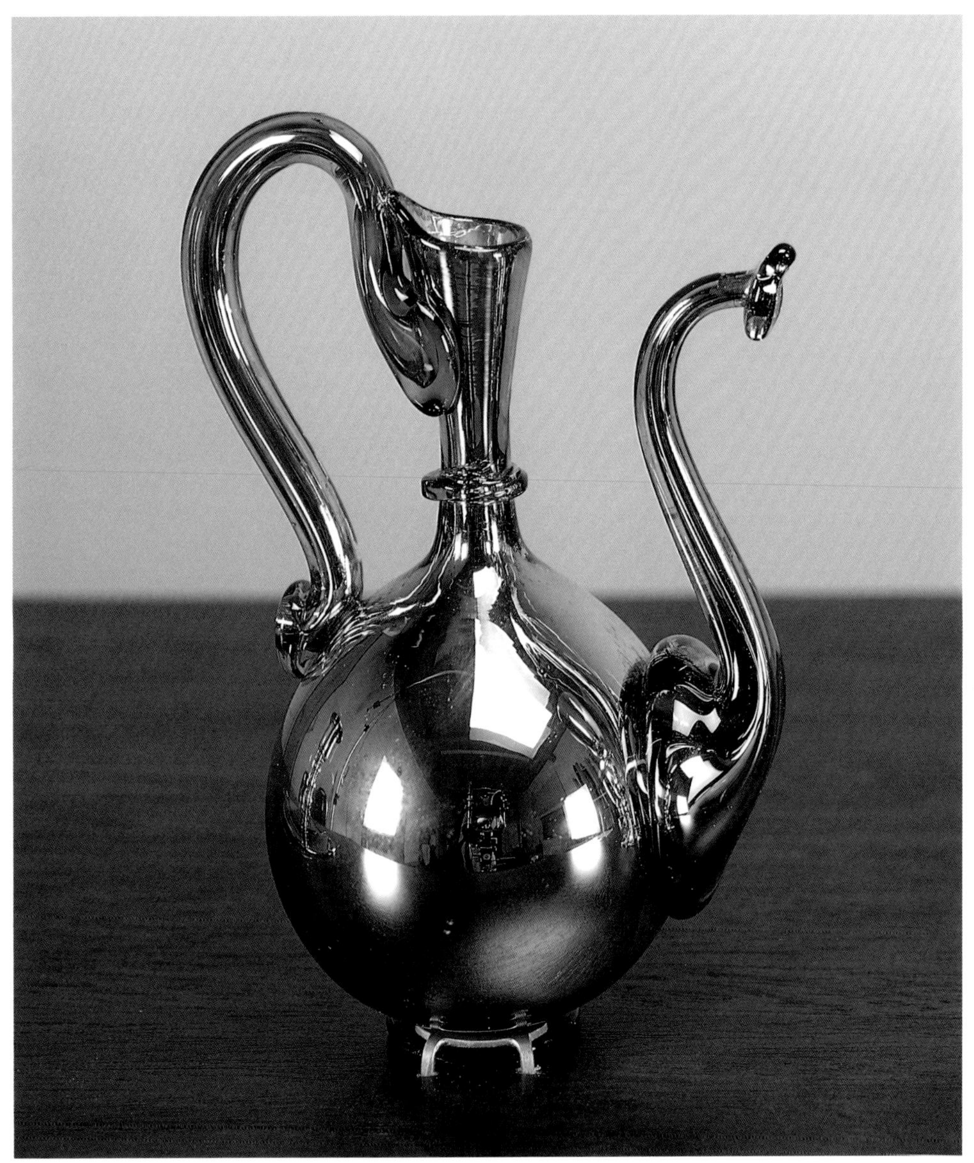

Acknowledgments

I would like to thank Director Anne Hawley, the staff of the Gardner Museum, and especially Jennifer Gross for their support of this exhibition and my residency at the Museum. Special thanks to the Massachusetts College of Art; AC Project Room, New York, New York; and the Donald Young Gallery, Chicago, Illinois, for their generosity and support.

Josiah McElheny

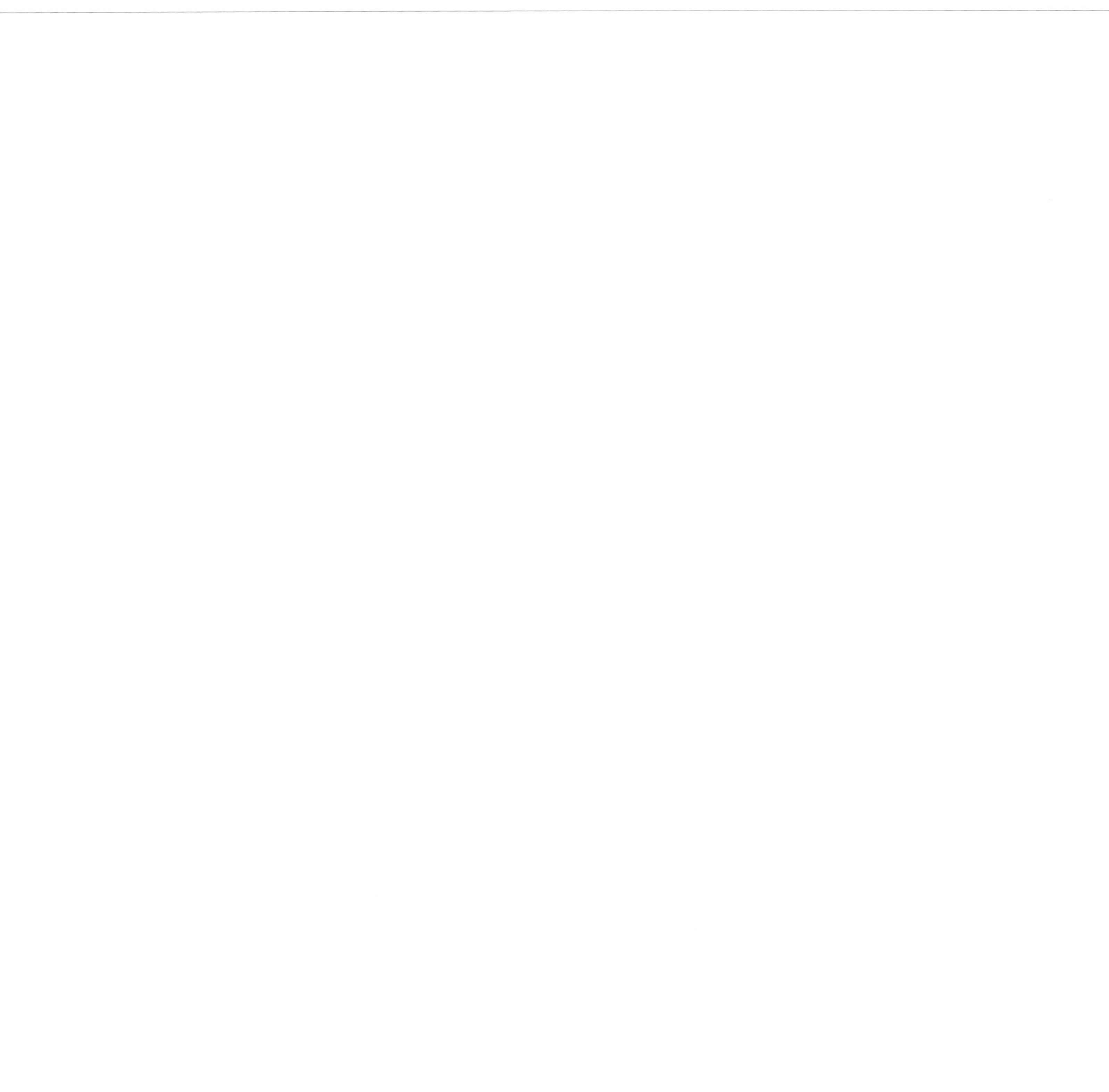

Foreword

In the fall of 1998, the Gardner Museum welcomed Josiah McElheny as an artist in residence. This catalog is the first publication devoted solely to Josiah McElheny and focuses not only on the new work inspired by the Gardner but also serves as a retrospective of his career.

Supporting the work of living artists and extending that work to our audiences is a major commitment of the Gardner Museum. In doing so, we continue the tradition begun by the Museum's founder, Isabella Stewart Gardner. It is our hope that the presentation of ideas contained in the visual object will help us understand our time as well as provide aesthetic pleasure to viewers.

The Museum is grateful to all those who made the exhibition—and Josiah McElheny's residency—possible: Jennifer R. Gross, curator of contemporary art and public programs, for curating Josiah McElheny's exhibition and residency; and Rebecca Jaskow, public programs coordinator, for organizing his work at the Museum.

We are thankful to art critic and professor Dave Hickey for his insightful essay. He makes issues of beauty and the value of art into conversations for all to enter.

We would like to thank the Glass Department at the Massachusetts College of Art for making their extraordinary facilities available to Josiah McElheny while in residency at the Gardner and for giving him the opportunity to share his experience and skills as a glassblower with the college's students.

Special thanks also go to Karen Croff Bates, curator of education; Gretchen Dietrich, assistant curator of education; and Linda Graetz, director of curriculum and instruction, for their commitment to realizing excellence in exhibition-related education programs. We also thank the teachers, students, and administrators who are our school partners in these programs.

Gratitude is in order to Susan Sinclair, archivist; Patrick McMahon, registrar and assistant to the chief curator of collections; and Isabelle Eaton, collections assistant, for access to the archives and for consistently bringing points of interest in the galleries into focus for the Museum's resident artists and "Eye of the Beholder" lecturers. Special thanks to Chris Aldrich, preparator; and Ruth Abrahams, designer. McElheny's experience of the Museum was also greatly enhanced by the dialogue and information shared with him by the conservators of the Museum, particularly chief conservator Barbara Mangum. We want also to thank the Museum's Security staff for facilitating his movement throughout the Museum grounds.

The Museum's programs are enriched through the oversight and support of the Museum's Program Committee, chaired by Barbara Lee, whose members include trustees Frieda Garcia and Beth Pfeiffer McNay and overseers Joanne Dickinson, Sheryl Foti-Strauss, Robert Freeman, Vivien Hassenfeld, Barbara Jordan, and David Scudder.

Sponsorship of artist programming is made possible by the Barbara Lee Program Fund. Major support for "Eye of the Beholder" programs has been provided by The Pew Charitable Trusts, the Stratford Foundation, The Boston Foundation, GTE, and the Clipper Ship Foundation.

A portion of the Museum's program operating funds for this fiscal year has also been provided through grants from the Institute of Museum and Library Services, a Federal agency; and the Massachusetts Cultural Council, a state agency that also receives support from the National Endowment for the Arts.

Anne Hawley, Director

INTRODUCTION

My first encounter with Josiah McElheny's work occurred shortly after I began my tenure as the contemporary curator at the Gardner Museum. The exhibition entitled "Non-Decorative Beautiful Objects" presented seemingly historical objects within the context of a contemporary art gallery. The show clarified a number of questions that had been circulating in my mind about the Museum and its collection rather than about McElheny's work. The truths exemplified in his exhibition appeared self-evident despite its pretense as fiction.

My questions had primarily focused on the increased value attributed to objects that were linked to history or a historical narrative, a subject resonant in the minds of many of us who work at the Museum. Working in the gap between the physical life of the collection and the mystifying reality of its history, one often feels suspended between the popular perception of the Museum as a cultural cliché of Isabella Gardner's fancy, museum and personal monument, and the exponential sum of its value as a compendium of art histories: Italian Renaissance, Gothic, Greek, American, etc.

As the months passed and my intimacy with Josiah McElheny's work and the collection increased, the ore of truth in my inquiry was refined by experience. In both cases, the narratives or meanings passed away, and I was left to the truth of objects, the authenticity of my experience of the Gardner: the weighty presence of the mortar and bricks of a grand palazzo, the sunlight that cuts through the atrium and is transformed into aromatic, moist air, and the tenderness in Giotto's *Presentation of the Infant Jesus in the Temple*. And in the case of McElheny's glassworks, I am left with the clarity in *Recreating a Miraculous Object*, the hope expressed in *Verzelini's Acts of Faith*, and the beauty in *Studies in the Search for Infinity*.

Josiah McElheny's work confirms a tradition of shared physical experience over transcribed knowledge that is affirmed in Isabella Gardner's motto regarding this Museum and its history: *"Pense Moult, Parle Peu, Ecris Rien"*—"Think Much, Say Little, Write Nothing." In the end, there is little to be said about truth; like glass, its value is in its clarity.

Jennifer R. Gross, Curator of Contemporary Art and Public Programs

Josiah McElheny: Hearts of Glass

Josiah McElheny: Hearts of Glass

If you ask Josiah McElheny about the autobiographical precedents for his curious obsession with fictional, factual artifacts—for some source of its technical and conceptual eccentricity—he mentions a semester in high school, before he began his arduous apprenticeship in the discipline of glass. During this period McElheny and his friends, to amuse themselves, would recount Jorge Luis Borges' *Ficciones* aloud to one another, conversationally, anecdotally, as if they were gossip. McElheny no longer remembers the precise occasion for this schoolboy diversion, but there is no denying that it was well-designed to demonstrate and perpetuate Borges' vision of the fluid, procreative relationship between talk and text, between one language and another, fiction and fact, dreams and history.

Most presciently McElheny's schoolboy exercise in "speaking Borges" incarnates the word; it translates the permanent, distanced, designative signage of the text into the intimate, ephemeral, embodied iconicity of the spoken word, thus setting Borges' imagined stories free in the physical world as entities in their own right, subject to the world's contingencies. This ontological action and direction—this motion from the text (or the picture) toward the hard fictions of the world—continues to characterize McElheny's artistic interests today. He is always moving from the word-in-text toward the word-incarnate, concerned less with the materialist disjunction of dreams and things than with the dreams that stuff is made of. McElheny makes this transit from the word-as-sign to sign-as-icon in his own diffident way, but he shares this alchemical concern with Andy Warhol and Jasper Johns. All three artists, while accepting the precedence of language as the material of culture, are most interested in the procreative consequences of language as visible speech, as a thing in the world.

McElheny's *Verzelini's Acts of Faith (Glass from paintings of the life of Christ)*, 1996, is a set piece demonstration of this agenda. *Verzelini's Acts of Faith* consists of thirty-seven glass objects presented in an antique display cabinet. As a Warhol Marilyn incarnates a printed, photographic image or a Jasper Johns flag incarnates a public idea, each object in McElheny's cabinet is an incarnation of a painted image. McElheny's objects, however, come to us cloaked in a secondary Borgesian narrative. Each does, in fact, embody an image of a piece of glassware that appears in a Renaissance painting that portrays an occasion in the life of Christ, but the glass objects themselves are presented to us as part of a historical narrative, as the creations of Giacamo Verzelini, an actual, historical, Venetian glassblower who worked in Venice, Antwerp and London and, thus, could have seen the paintings in which this glassware appears. According to McElheny's appended narrative, Verzelini created these objects not as exercises in form or craft or scientific representations, but as acts of devotion.

The artistic inferences that may be drawn from McElheny's *ficciones* are multifarious, of course. On the level of craft, *Verzelini's Acts of Faith* may be taken as an effort to relocate the practice of making blown glass within the intellectual tradition of Western art making—to create for it a kind of Borgesian, parallel history, a rhetoric of sources and echoes, which in true Borgesian fashion (given the whims of history and the fragility of glass) may have actually existed. Or certainly could have.

In *Studies in the Search for Infinity*, McElheny creates a series of plates that serves the same purpose. The first plates in this series accommodate the decorative motifs of Renaissance artifacts to the rhetoric of Renaissance perspectival geometry, its speculative representations of infinity. The last plate in this series is a literalized evocation of the same iconography—a descending spiral captured as a pattern of bubbles in the glass.

In this manner, *Studies in the Search for Infinity* simultaneously incarnates and narrates the infinite regression of history while inferring a secret history of glassware that declares its appropriateness to just the sort of scientific and metaphysical speculation that informed picture making in the Renaissance. By this fictional fiat, McElheny inserts the practice of blown glass into the Western beaux-arts tradition at very nearly the moment that the secrets of blown glass were reintroduced into European practice after a long medieval hiatus. Subsequently, in his "modernizations" of traditional glassware, McElheny imagines glass participating in the vertiginous, ideological dialectic of frictionless, beaux-arts style change that derived from these Renaissance models and their insistence on style-as-argument. In one of these "modernizations," McElheny updates a design by Adolph Loos, who thought of ornament as crime, with ornamental flowers.

McElheny, however, is less concerned with reasserting the "respectability" of glass as an "intellectual" artistic medium in the history of art than with speculating on the implications of considering it as such—considering what glass does and how it is done. As a consequence, McElheny's recent work, by embodying concepts rather than conceptualizing glass, may be considered as part of a broader artistic movement aimed at reasserting the sources of representation in ornamental practice—in the red and black narrative on the Greek wine cup, the wolf's heads on the handle of the Gothic dagger, and the erotic cartouche on the Florentine wedding chest. This reconsideration of the function of representation, of course, involves a reconsideration of the function of art, which in many ways echoes John Ruskin's antimodernist insistence that "all great art is praise"—his assumption that we human beings create objects, structures, institutions and occasions because we need them and that we make them well so they will last, then ornament them because we love what we have made and we love what these objects and institutions do and mean.

By relocating representation in the practice of ornamenting objects, ideas and occasions of social and cultural value, McElheny is not alone in his effort to strip away the scientistic assumptions of Enlightenment realism and rewrite representation as a secondary, nonautonomous practice of celebration and devotion—as "a discourse of love," in Oleg Grabar's phrase. Beginning with Pollock and Warhol, artists as disparate as Robert Gober, Jeff Koons, Robert Zakanitch and Philip Taaffe have each in their own way asserted the ornamental priority and function of image making. In doing so, they have reasserted the Mediterranean sources of that tradition, its roots in the iconophile tendencies of its antique and modern civilizations. (To cite the simplest example, Jeff Koons' kitsch-pornographic paintings of himself and his Italian porn-star/politician wife echo exactly, in a slightly higher key, the erotic content of the Renaissance decorative paintings designed to decorate the bedchambers of newlyweds.) In this sense, when McElheny and his colleagues in the practice of ornament ground their practice in the mysteries of Renaissance production and speculation, they do not so much activate the history of Western art as short-circuit its progress, eliding its divagation into the Protestant north by constructing etiology that leads directly from Venice to the New World.

The most critical implication of McElheny's recreated narrative of art and glass, however, is his inference that it is, in one sense, true—simply because the history of making blown glass is an oral and physical tradition transmitted by the laying on of hands and spoken words. So, even though McElheny is not Verzelini, Verzelini is in him. They are absolutely connected in the living history of the practice. And it is this incarnate history of talk and touch that constitutes a large part of McElheny's interest in what he does. The skills required to make blown glass reside within a single, secretive oral tradition. They have been passed down from master to apprentice over the centuries and continue to be. Thus, McElheny's ongoing education with master glassblowers Ronald Wilkinson, Jan-Erik Ritzman and, most recently, Lino Tagliapietra is the farthest thing from the standardized "text-learning" of institutionalized liberal education; McElheny and his mentors are engaged in the passing on of mysteries that all derive from a single source.

Unlike the practice of making clay objects or even painting, the making of blown glass is not a multisource practice. It began, as far as anyone can tell, in the pharaonic kingdoms of Egypt and was dispersed within the diaspora of Hellenistic culture to the Middle East and from there to Mediterranean Europe. It flourished there until the Middle Ages, when it died out in Europe until the fifteenth century, at which time Venetian travelers, merchants and craftsmen recovered the practice from the Middle East and passed it on in a single stream. So, the sense of physical inheritance that informs McElheny's work is as certain as it is undocumentable. The devotional exercise that McElheny attributes to Verzelini is not simply an imagined action. It is an internalized memory, and this empowers McElheny to "reenact" Verzelini's act of devotion in his own regional idiom, out of his own cultural iconography, in *The Abominable Tumbler*, by incarnating out of Herman Melville's words the "abominable" and deceptive tumblers from which Ishmael drinks at the beginning of the novel.

The most mysterious and Borgesian aspect of the tradition and practice of making blown glass, however, resides in the fact that it constitutes the perfect example of Baudriallard's "precession of the simulacra," since glass existed in language before it existed in the world. Its physical attributes—its aspects of transparency, translucency, reflection and refraction—probably existed for centuries before the material itself was created; it existed precisely as the self-describing rhetoric of thought and language itself. Upon its invention, then, glass almost inevitably took on the aspect of language and thought incarnate, defining them in its reflection. It may, indeed, have required the invention of glass as an objective correlative to think about thought or to speak about language in a truly critical way. In any case, the virtues and imperfections of glass empower the vast majority of our insights into the virtues and imperfections of language: our ideas about the thoughtful sobriety and willful narcissism of self-reflection—our sense of language as a mirror—our doubled sense of disinterested, distanced speculation, its admirable curiosity and subliminal aggression, and most critically, our understanding of the limits and distortions of even the most apparent transparency.

It is the great virtue of Josiah McElheny's art that it dwells within and speculates relentlessly upon the eternal circularity of glass as object and idea—as the very emblem of human civilization in its stubborn hardness, its fictional transparency, and its extreme fragility. Like civilization itself, glass is destroyed only by violence. It does not wear away as stone and metal do, although its meaning, as an emblem of civilization's tough fragility, can wear away. As a consequence, the most modest and affecting of McElheny's works for me is *Recreating a Miraculous Object*. For this piece, the artist displays a reproduction of a fresco from Padua that depicts one of the Miracles of Saint Anthony, in which a glass cup purportedly fell from a bell tower and did not break. McElheny has reincarnated the glass cup from the fresco and exhibits it next to the fresco in reproduction. The peculiar effect of this piece, when we are confronted with the glass object and the pictorial narration, is that we know, somehow, that it didn't happen. Either the cup wasn't glass, or it didn't fall or, indeed, it fell and broke. McElheny's recreation of that glass, however, and his insistence of his position within the living tradition of the glassmaker who created the original glass, insists just as miraculously and even more poignantly upon the tough persistence of its living culture—of the makers and doers, the users and talkers who think in terms of glass.

Dave Hickey
Las Vegas

PLATES

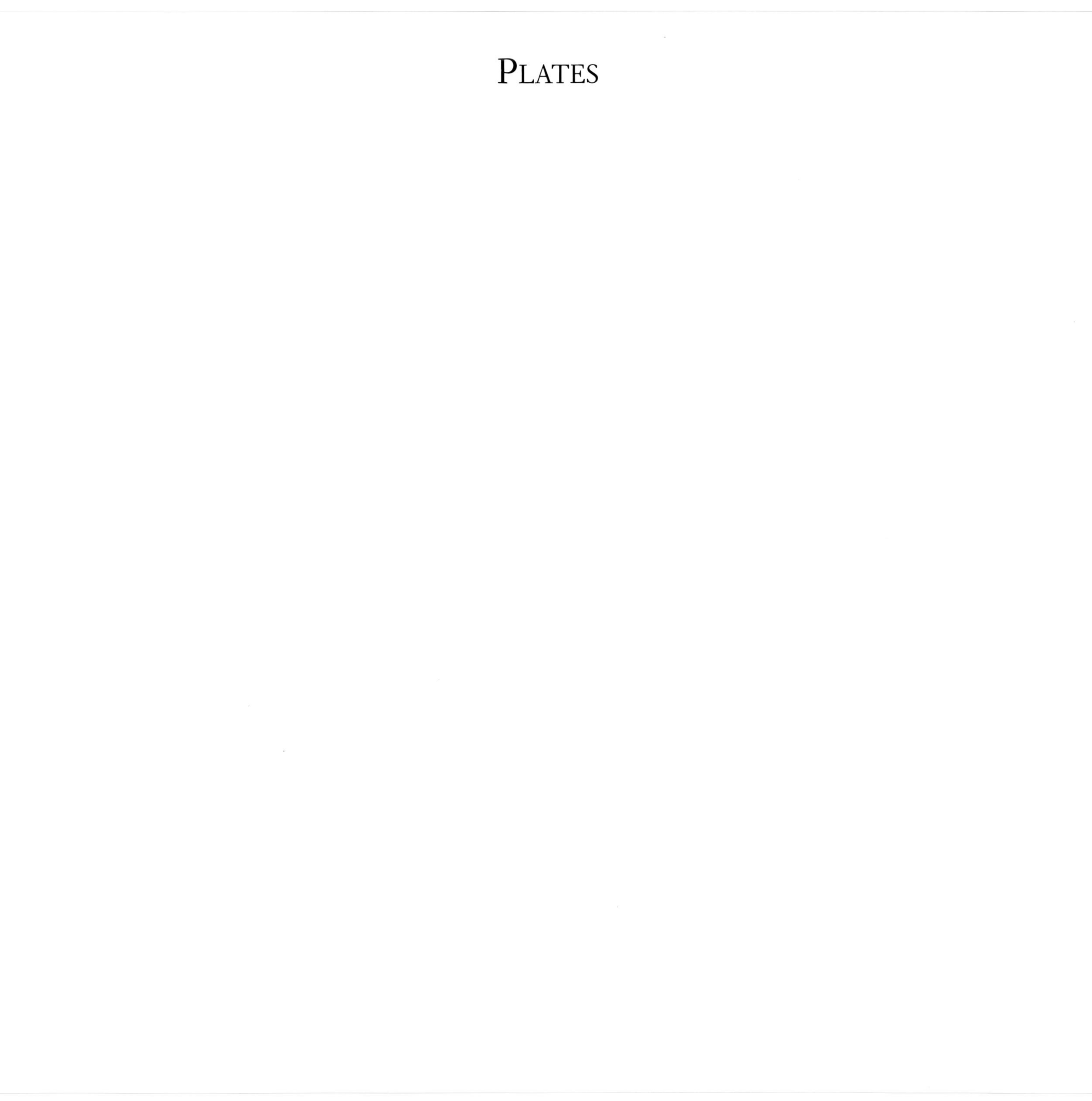

STUDIES IN THE SEARCH FOR INFINITY (detail)
Blown glass, display, and text
20 x 144 x 8 inches
1997–1998
The Saatchi Gallery, London

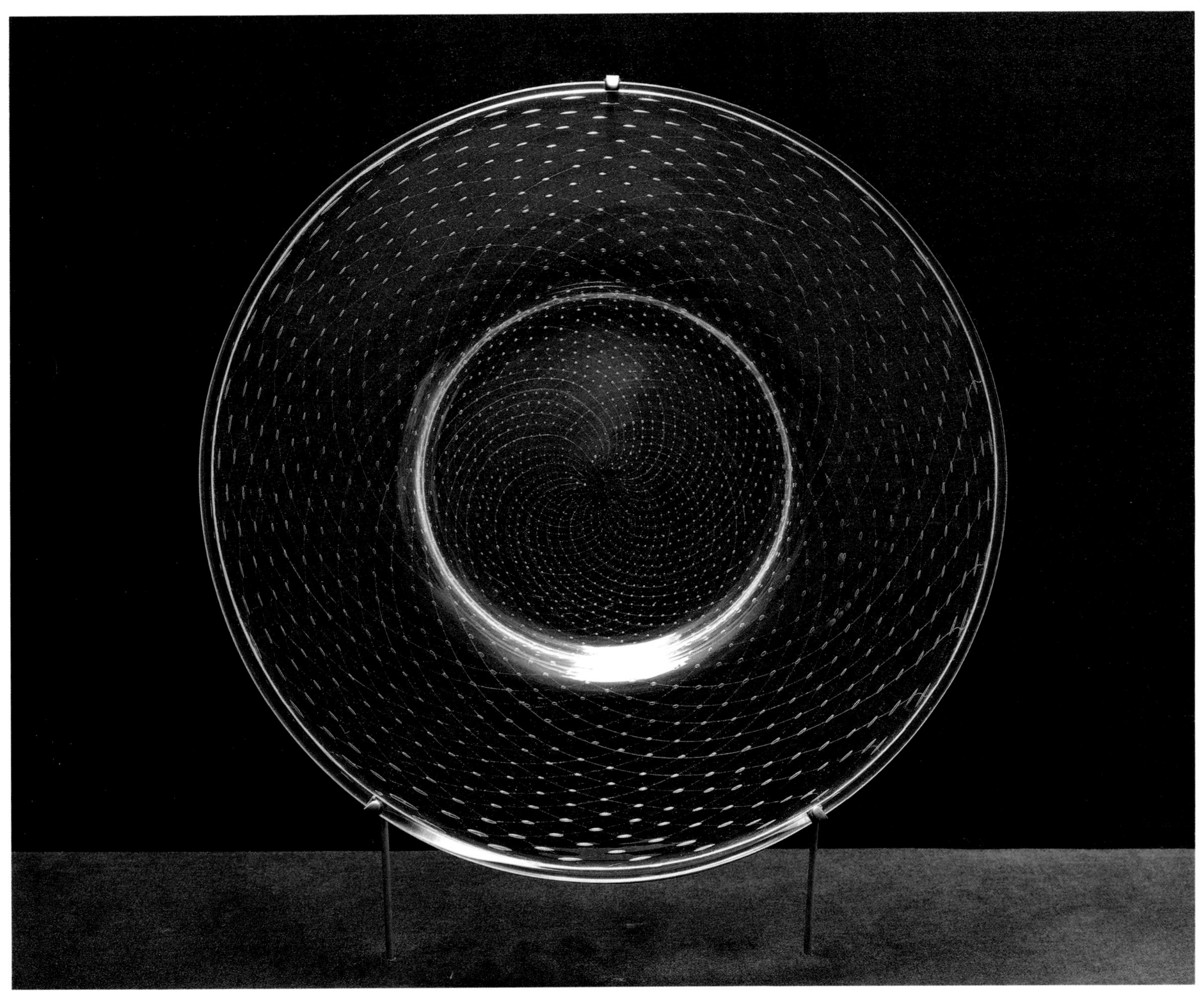

STUDIES IN THE SEARCH FOR INFINITY (overall view)
Blown glass, display, and text
20 x 144 x 8 inches
1997–1998
The Saatchi Gallery, London

The following is a copy of the text from the work

Studies in the Search for Infinity

   Perspective drawing was developed by painters of the Renaissance era. In their search for the spiritual perfection of image, painters devised various geometric methodologies for creating the illusion of three dimensional space. The point of infinity or vanishing point was the reference used to construct pictures in accordance with the laws of optics. Scholars of mathematics used these concrete visualizations to give the concept of infinity a precise meaning.

   In parallel with painting, Renaissance Venetian glassblowers aimed to depict a perfected, spiritually true reality through the use of point perspective. The appearance of infinite distance was created by elaborate patterning within the glass. These designs were generated by abstracting the geometric templates used to determine the relative proportion of objects within a picture plane. Great preparation and concentration was involved in creating patterns that formed the image of endlessness.

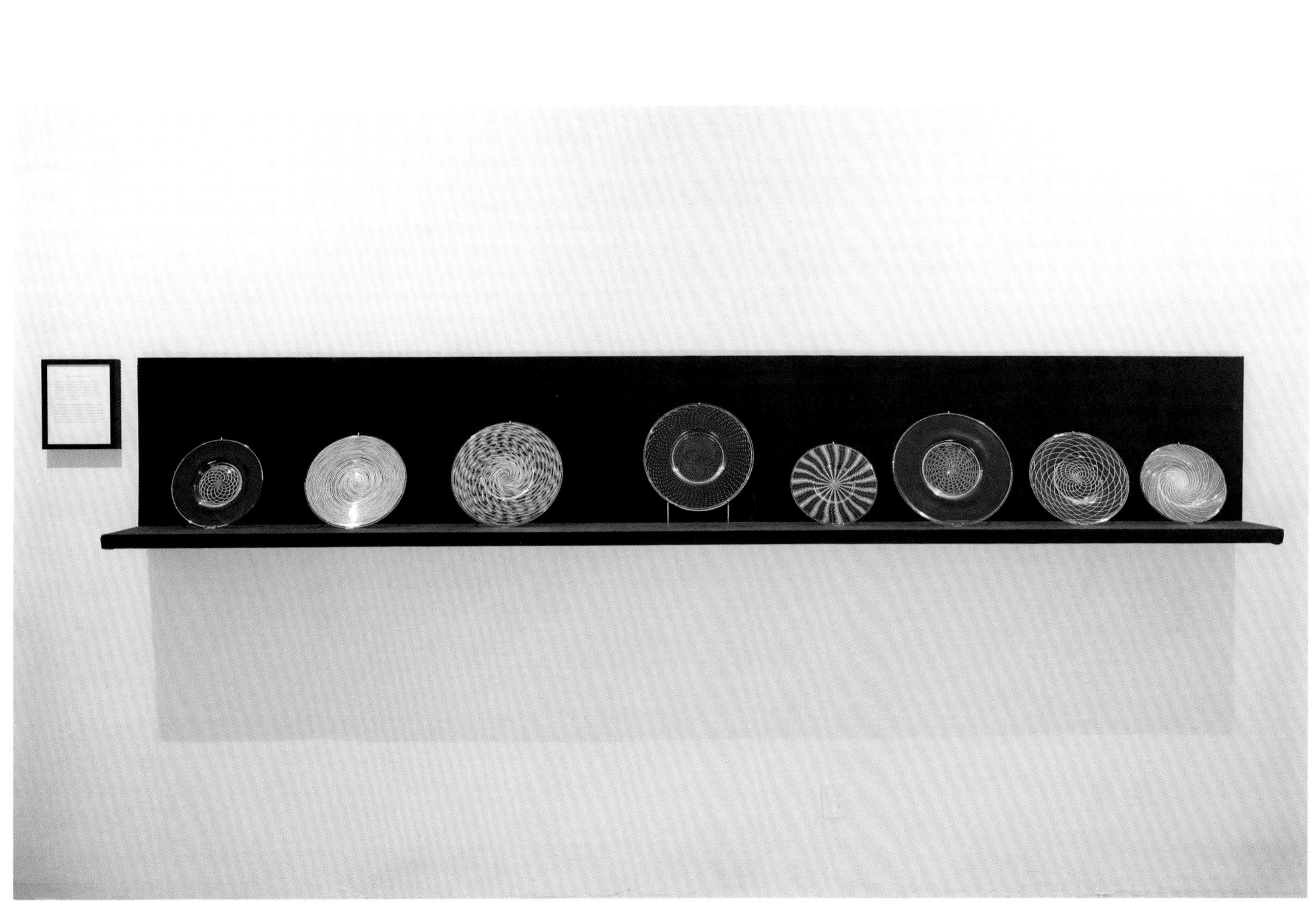

RECREATING A MIRACULOUS OBJECT
Blown glass, photography, display, and text
Object 10 x 10 x 11 inches, photograph 12 x 17 inches
1997
Courtesy AC Project Room, New York, New York

The following is a copy of the text from the work

This fresco from the sixteenth century depicts the "miracle of the cup," one of the miracles of Saint Anthony of Padua. The glass, which fell from the great heights of the bell tower, not only survived the fall but broke the pavement. Many people were in the square to witness the event.

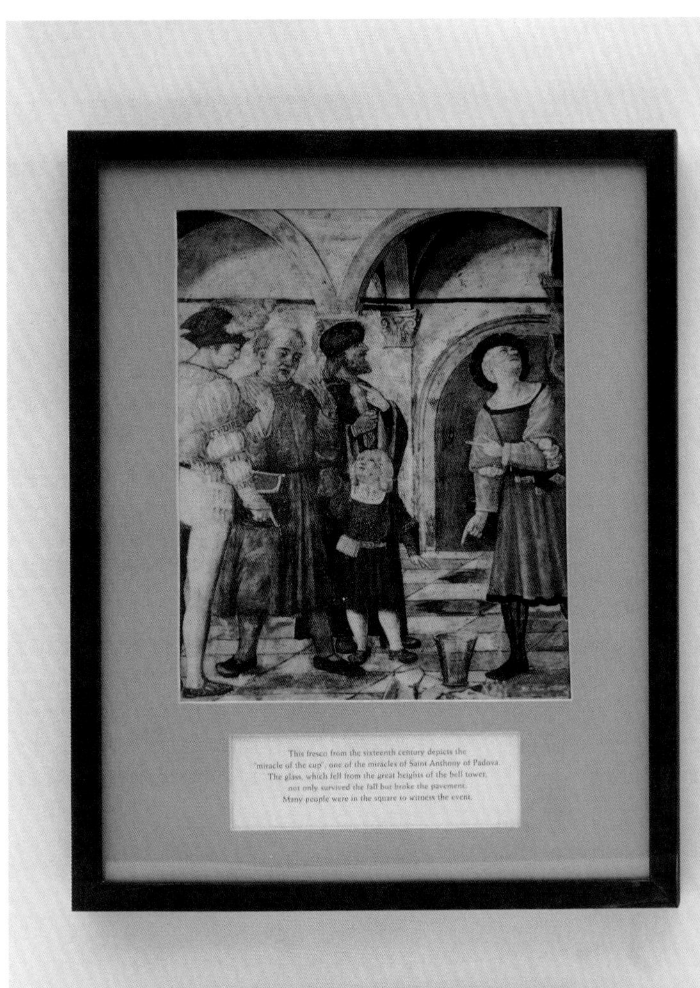

This fresco from the sixteenth century depicts the
'miracle of the cup', one of the miracles of Saint Anthony of Padova.
The glass, which fell from the great heights of the bell tower,
not only survived the fall but broke the pavement.
Many people were in the square to witness the event.

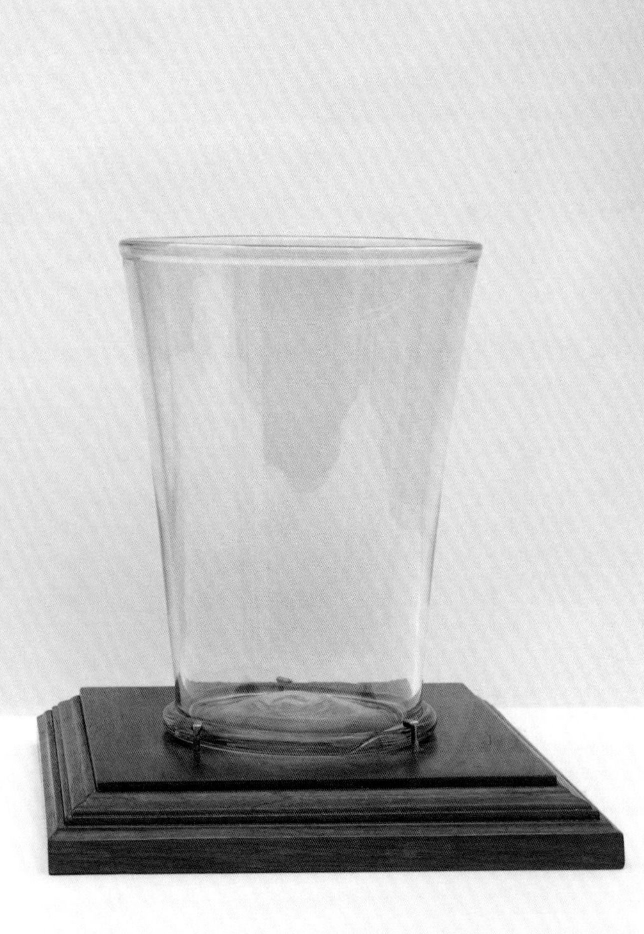

THE DEVELOPMENT OF SOCIAL CRITIQUE (THE DESIGNS OF JACOPO LIGOZZI)
Blown glass, drawing, text, and display
Dimensions variable
1996–1998
Courtesy of Donald Young Gallery, Chicago, Illinois; and AC Project Room, New York, New York

The following is a copy of the text from the work

The Development of Social Critique

Jacopo Ligozzi, court draftsman to Cosimo II of the Medici, began in 1617 to make drawings for the production of glass at the Florence factory in the Pitti Palace. Ligozzi had these three wine glasses made by Muranese master Giacomo Della Luna to point out the lengths that aristocrats would go to to define their own elegance. In this period it had become important to drink from glass as a part of an elite life of grace. Ligozzi consciously created these glasses both to fit into this lifestyle and to simultaneously critique it. It is virtually impossible to drink from these glasses without spilling wine on oneself. Through exaggeration, he used the object itself to insert his own concepts of rebellion and inquiry into the culture at large. This kind of object-based analysis of the social structure only returns with the art and design of the 20th century.

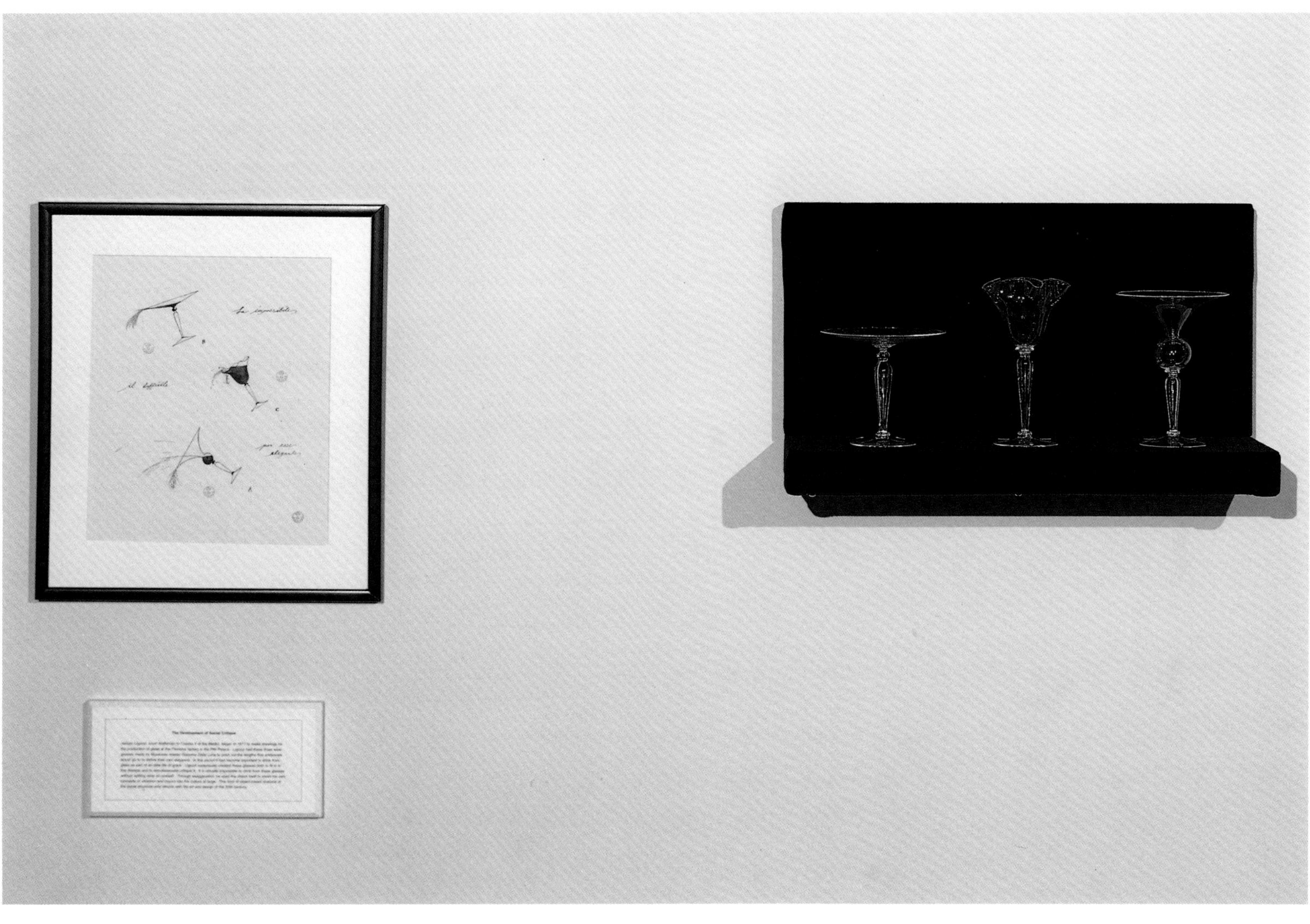

VERZELINI'S ACTS OF FAITH (GLASS FROM PAINTINGS OF THE LIFE OF CHRIST)
Blown glass, text, display
79 x 73 x 15 inches
1996
The Saatchi Gallery, London

The following is a selection of the text from the work

Verzelini's Acts of Faith
Glass from paintings of the life of Christ

The objects in this display were made by Giacomo Verzelini (1522–1606), a Venetian glassblower who worked in Venice, Antwerp, and London. Each object is a recreation of glass depicted in Renaissance and Medieval paintings of the life of Christ, which as a minor nobleman, he had seen in his travels in Europe. This group of objects was made not as an exploration of form but as an act of devotion, a way for the glassblower to become closer to the reality of his belief. These careful copies, known as "Verzelini's Acts of Faith," were made exclusively for his private religious veneration. They connected him to, and reinforced his belief in, the miraculous events of Christ's life. For him these objects were both symbols of the events and sensual relics.

We know little about Verzelini's life before his arrival in England. In 1574, soon after coming to London, Queen Elizabeth I granted Verzelini sole right and patent (an exclusive license) to produce Venetian-style glass in England. This proved so successful that Crutched Friars, his first glass factory, was soon burned to the ground by his frustrated English rivals. After he retired, his sons Francis and Jacob were jailed for ten years for trying to continue their father's business. However, he recovered to live as a prosperous and well loved man until his death in 1606. Throughout his life, in addition to his commercial work, he continued this work to honor his faith.

THE ANNUNCIATION, *top shelf*
A glass vessel near the angel and Mary in these Annunciation paintings is a symbol for the body as a receptacle for the soul. The vase frequently holds a lily, representing virginity, an olive branch, representing peace, or a carnation, representing pure love.

From left to right, from the paintings by: Pieter Huys, Lorenzo Costa and Benvenuto Tisi, Paolo Veronese

THE LAST SUPPER, *third shelf*
These paintings show the glass cups, decanters, and plates used for wine and bread. In different versions the table is set either with glass for each disciple or with shared vessels.

From left to right, from the paintings by: Mechtelt toe Boecop, Tintoretto (four objects), Joos van Cleve (three objects), Paolo Veneziano, Gerolamo Romanino

THE SUPPER AT EMMAUS, *bottom shelf*
Glass is at the table in these paintings of the resurrected Christ eating in the village of Emmaus after he was finally recognized by his disciples.

Starting from the second from the left, from left to right, from paintings by: Caravaggio (two objects), an Anonymous Venetian, Paolo Veronese, Tintoretto, an Anonymous Florentine painter, Vincenzo Catena

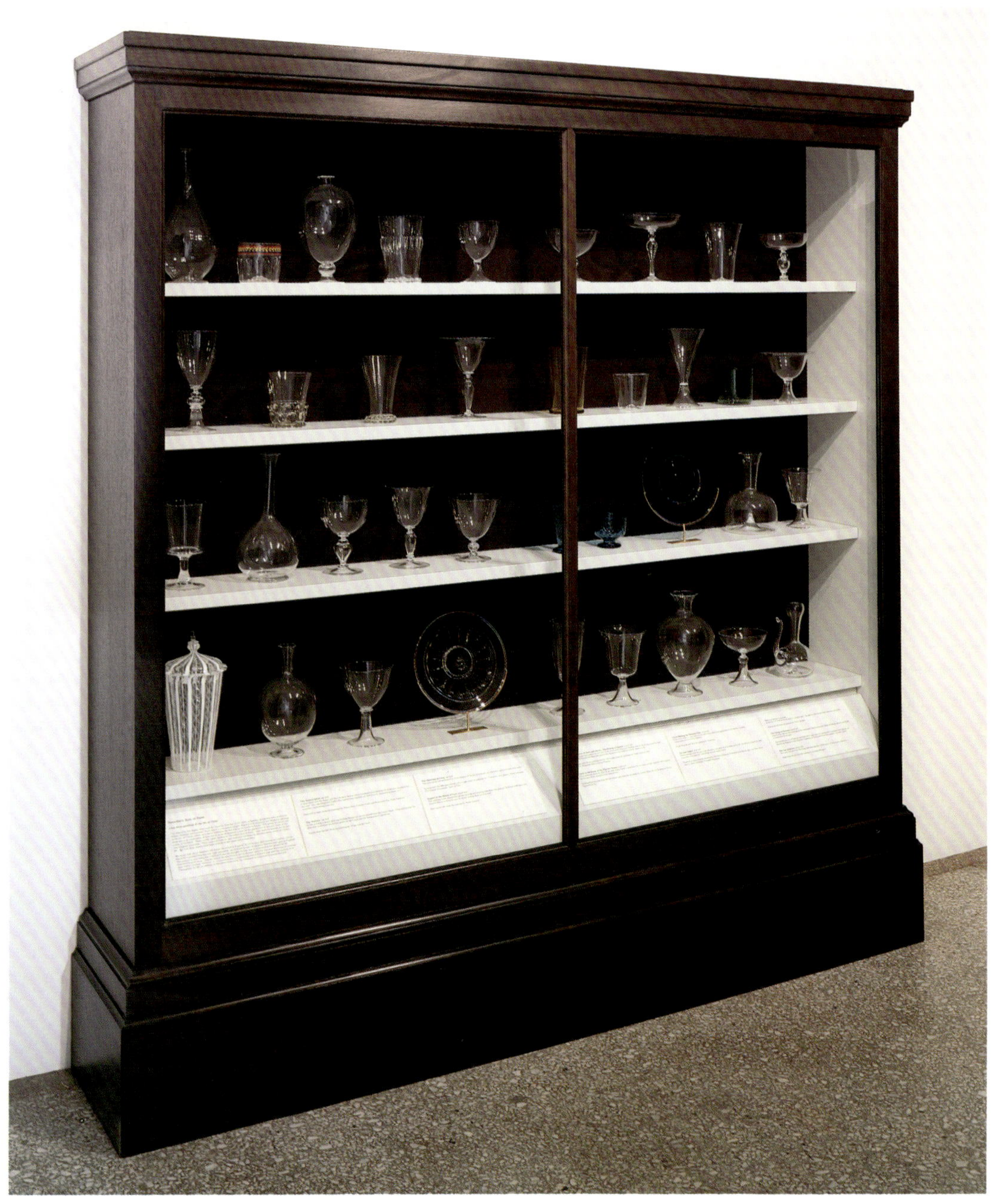

HISTORY MODERNIZED
Fifteen glass objects, fifteen photographs, text, and display
Dimensions variable
1998
The Saatchi Gallery, London

The following is an example of the captions in each of the photographs

Goblet, c. 1675
Engraved blown glass, the Netherlands
Collection of the Art Institute of Chicago

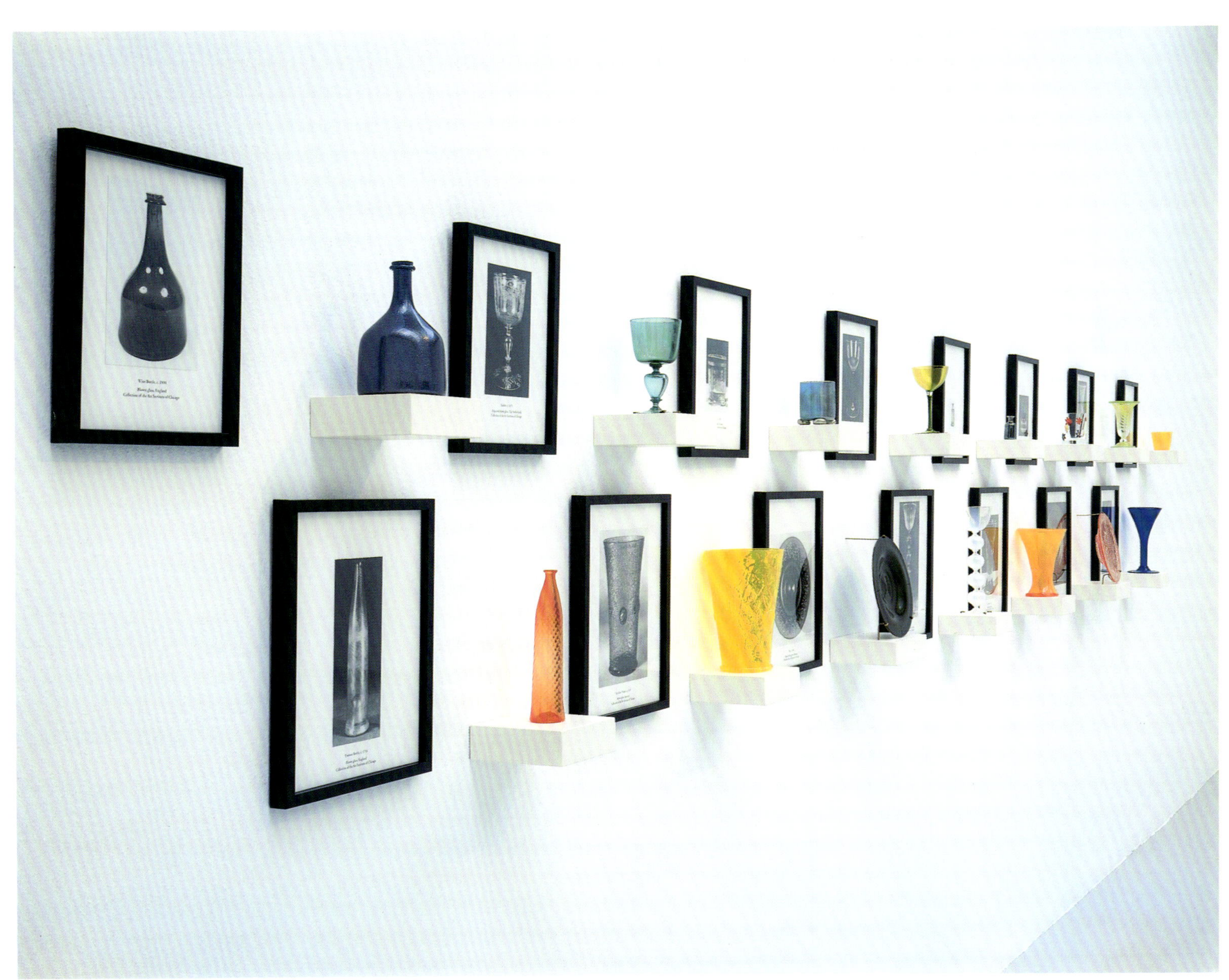

THE LAST SUPPER ACCORDING TO LEONARDO DA VINCI
AND THE LAST SUPPER ACCORDING TO JOSIAH MCELHENY
Blown glass, drawing, text, and display
24 x 102 x 6 inches
1997
Courtesy AC Project Room, New York, New York

The following is a copy of the text from the work

The Last Supper According to Leonardo da Vinci
and The Last Supper According to Josiah McElheny

   In paintings of the Last Supper, the cups from which the disciples drink play a central role. Medieval and Renaissance painters often chose to depict these cups as glass vessels, possibly because of the spiritual metaphors the material implied. The artist attempted to present an accurate vision of the historical event, even though they frequently used objects from their own era in the paintings.

   Leonardo da Vinci's painting of the Last Supper includes twelve simple glass cups on the table in front of Christ and the disciples. Josiah McElheny's version of the Last Supper consists of cups based on glass that is known to have been made in the first half of the first century in Palestine. During this period, glass was in common use throughout the Roman Empire, and was so inexpensive that people of all classes used it regularly in everyday life.

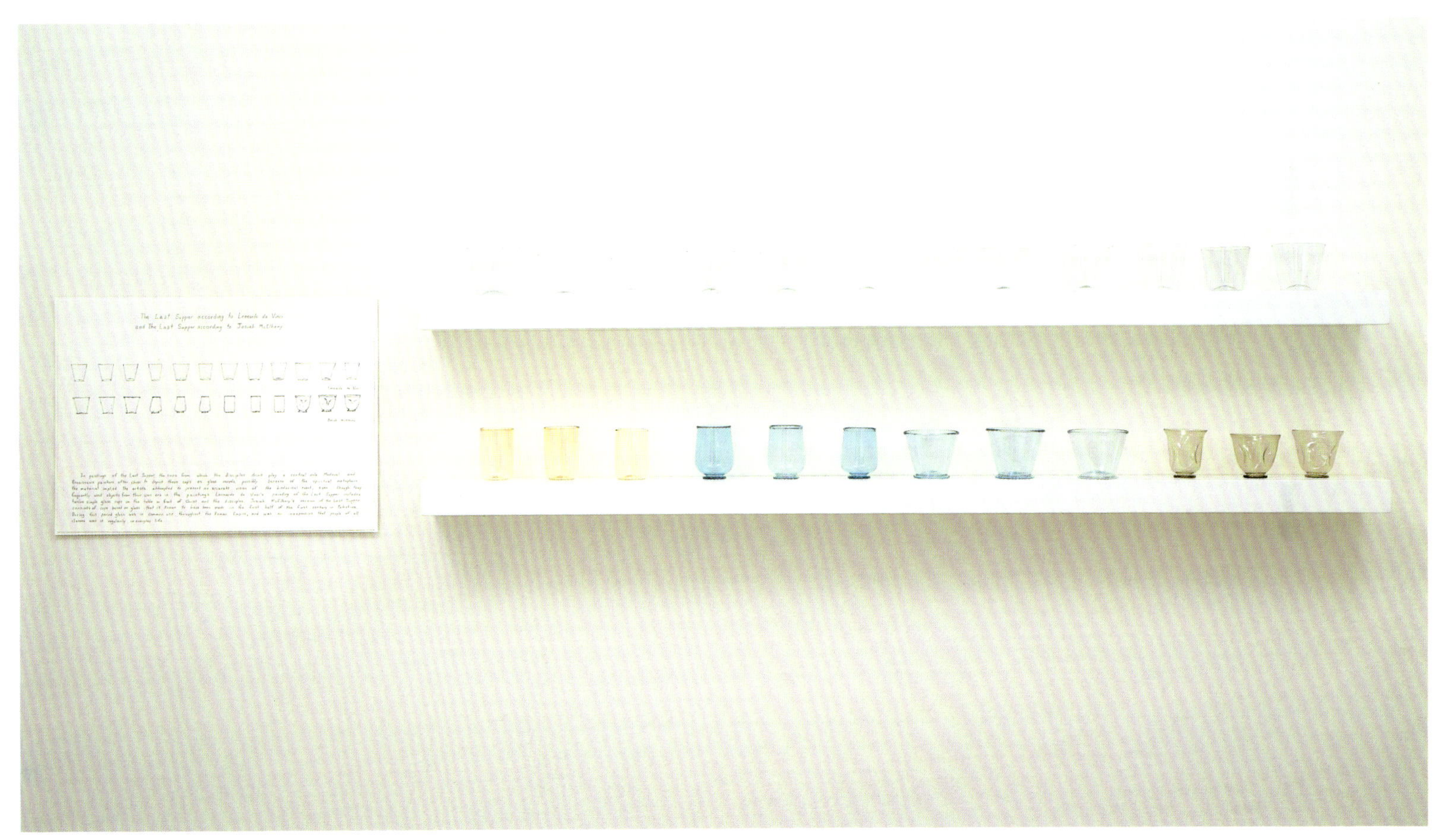

THE CONTROVERSY SURROUNDING THE "VERONESE" VASE
(FROM THE OFFICE OF LUIGI ZECCHIN)
Blown glass, metal shelving, bulletin board, drawings, and text
Dimensions variable
1996
Collection of the Museum of Contemporary Art, San Diego, California

The following is a copy of the text from the work

The Controversy Surrounding the "Veronese Vase"
From the office of Luigi Zecchin

Luigi Zecchin (1905–1984) was possibly the greatest historian to specialize in Italian glass. Trained as a civil engineer, he was professor of actuarial mathematics at Venice University. His passion for glass began when he apprenticed in his uncle's glass factory as a child. He later devoted his free time to becoming an expert on the regulations, laws, and statues of the historical glass industry, and was widely published.

As a tribute to his dedication we have displayed here one of his final projects. This work concerns the vase known as the "Veronese," which was designed by the painter Vittorio Zecchin, Luigi's uncle, for the Cappellin Venini Company in the 1920's. He had based it on the vessel in Paolo Veronese's version of the Annunciation, hanging in Venice's Gallerie dell' Accademia. In its simplicity it represented a break from the overly baroque Renaissance revival that had dominated Venice during the preceding fifty years. The "Veronese" became an icon of Venice's past grand traditions of glass, and various workshops copied it.

A controversy gradually arose among the glassblowers on Murano as to the exact shape of the vessel in the painting. Luigi Zecchin, who took it upon himself to find a definitive answer, began by collecting the interpretations of the vessel shown here. Then he returned to the painting itself. In order to convey its transparency, Veronese had painted each side of the vessel differently. Luigi Zecchin calculated a complete form based first on the vessel's left side, then on the right side, and finally on a mathematical average of the two. He commissioned a glassblower to make versions based on these drawings, the result of which are also exhibited here. None of the three exactly resembles the vessel in the painting.

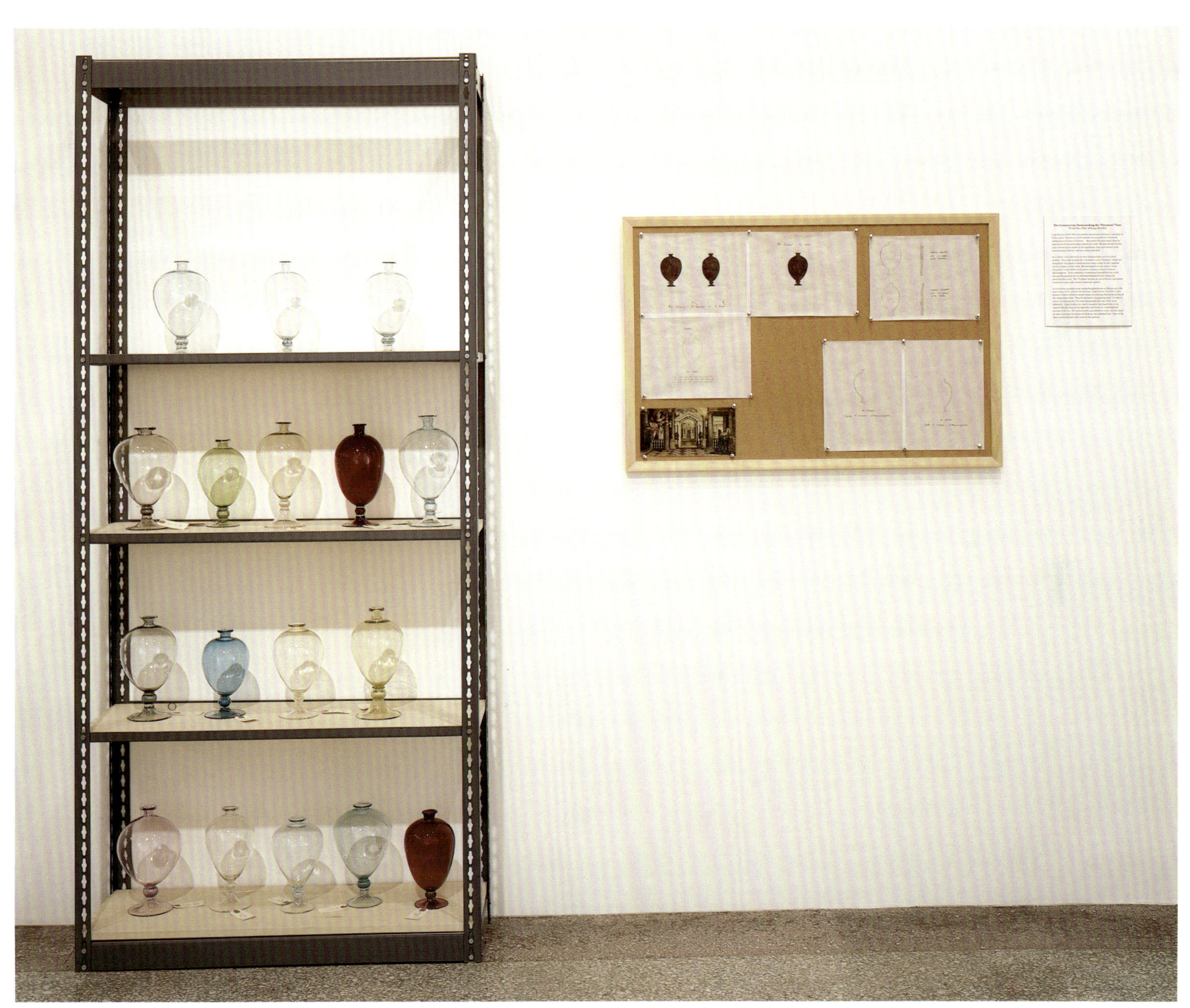

CHURCH SERVICE FOR POOR PEOPLE
Silvered blown glass, text, display
71 x 44 x 18 inches
1998
Courtesy the Artist, AC Project Room, New York, New York; and Donald Young Gallery, Chicago, Illinois

The following is a selection of the text from the work

Church Service for Poor People

   This glass service belongs to the tradition called 'poor man's silver', in which hollow glass is mirrored in imitation of sterling silver. 'Poor man's silver' was much less expensive, but it was also infinitely more fragile and ephemeral. Beginning in the 19th century it was found in many impoverished households. The church service and altar table here were donated by Italian glassblowers in a holiday offering for the poor. The local priest had insisted that the glass-workers make a gift for a church that only served the indigent.

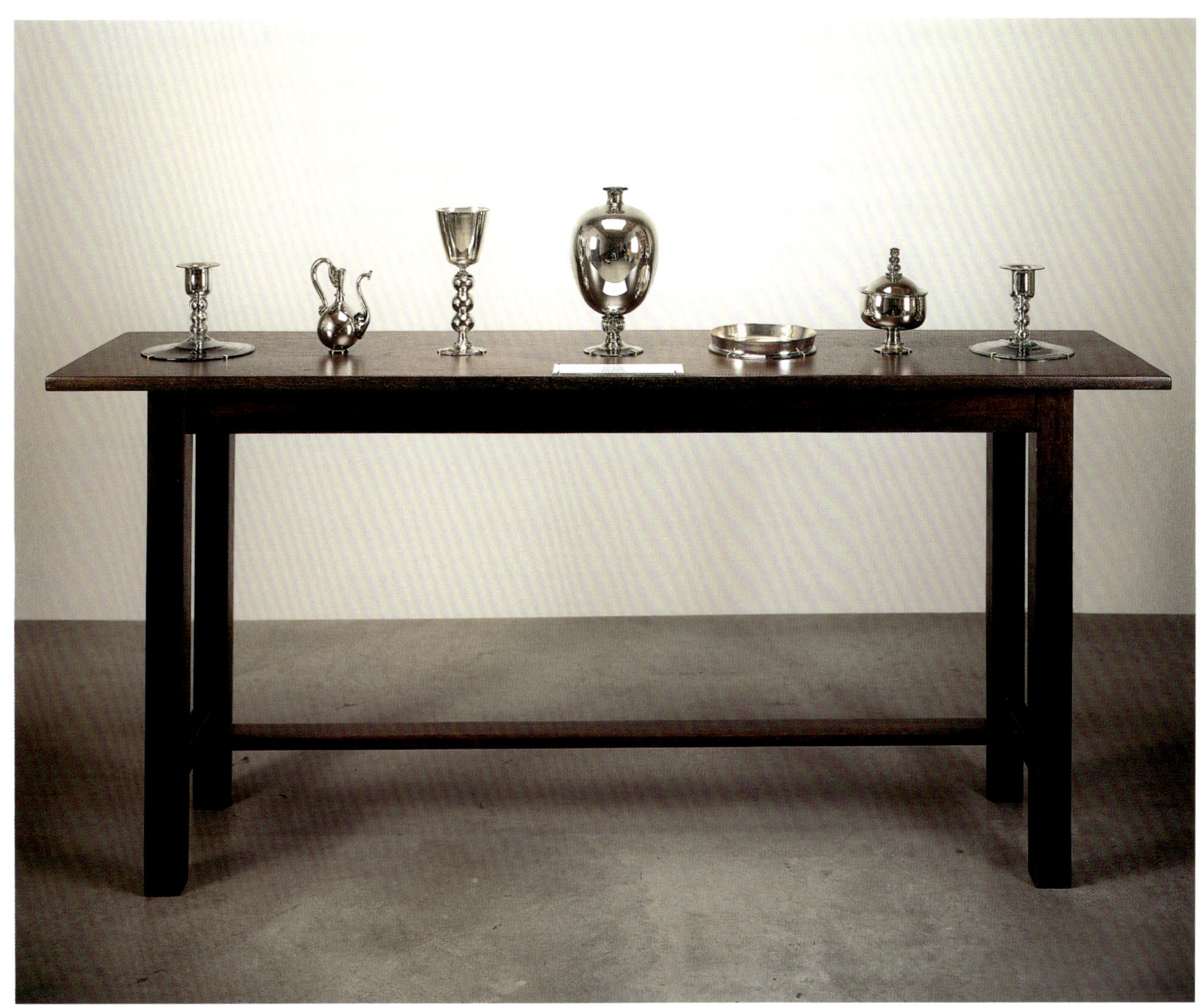

HISTORY OF MIRRORS
Silvered blown glass, display
Dimensions variable
1998
Courtesy the Artist, AC Project Room, New York, New York; and Donald Young Gallery, Chicago, Illinois

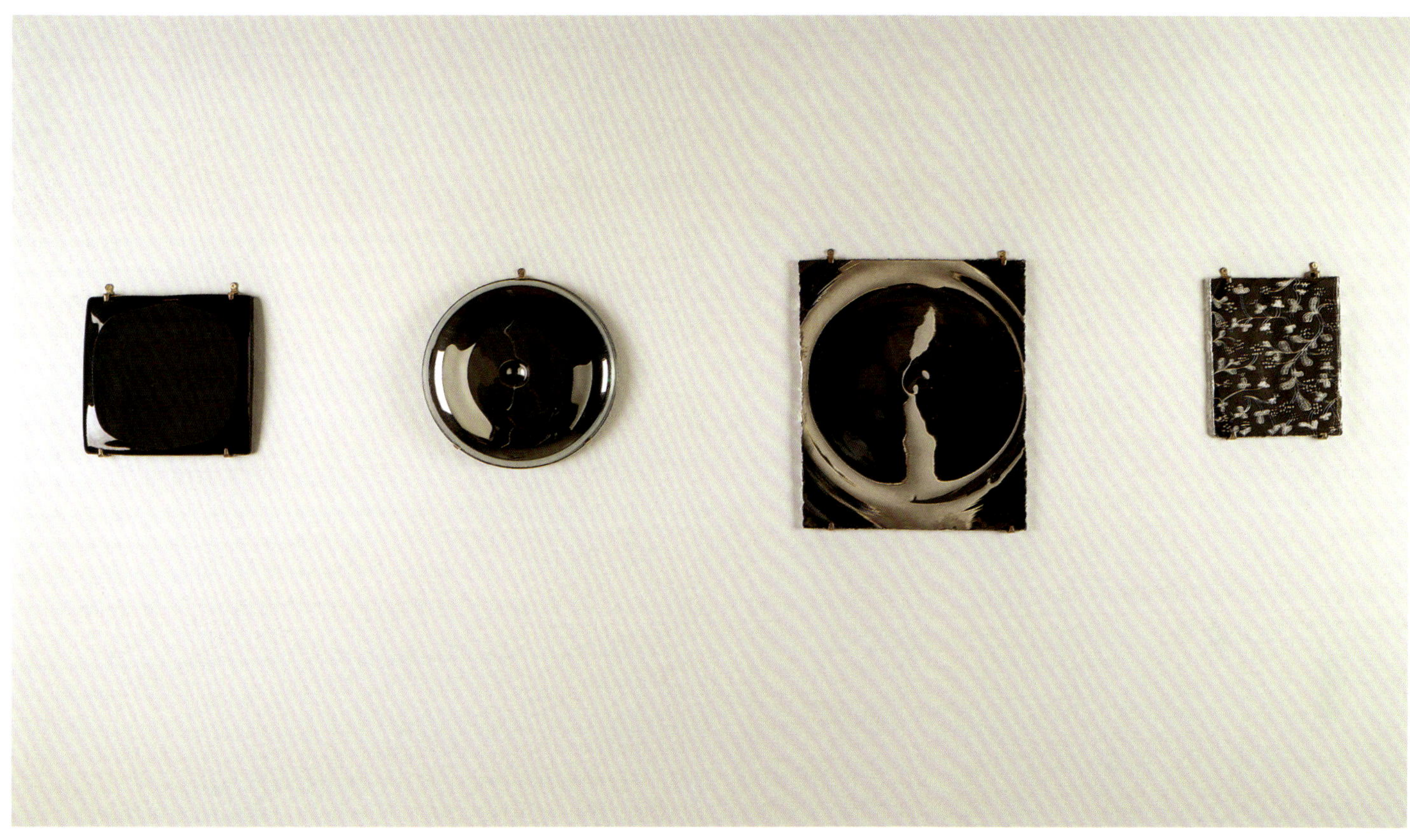

MEMORY (TWO SISTERS)
Blown glass, text, display
13 x 17 x 14 inches
1995
Courtesy of Donald Young Gallery, Chicago, Illinois

The following is a copy of the text from the work

Memory
Two Sisters

   These two cosmetic jars were found in Herculaneum in a room with two beds and two matching cosmetic tables, one jar on each table. Because of this they are believed to have belonged to two sisters. These circumstances are recorded only because the excavator noted their location at the time of their discovery on two tags. From one of the earliest excavations of Herculaneum, it was not common practice during the pre-1860 excavations to record such details.

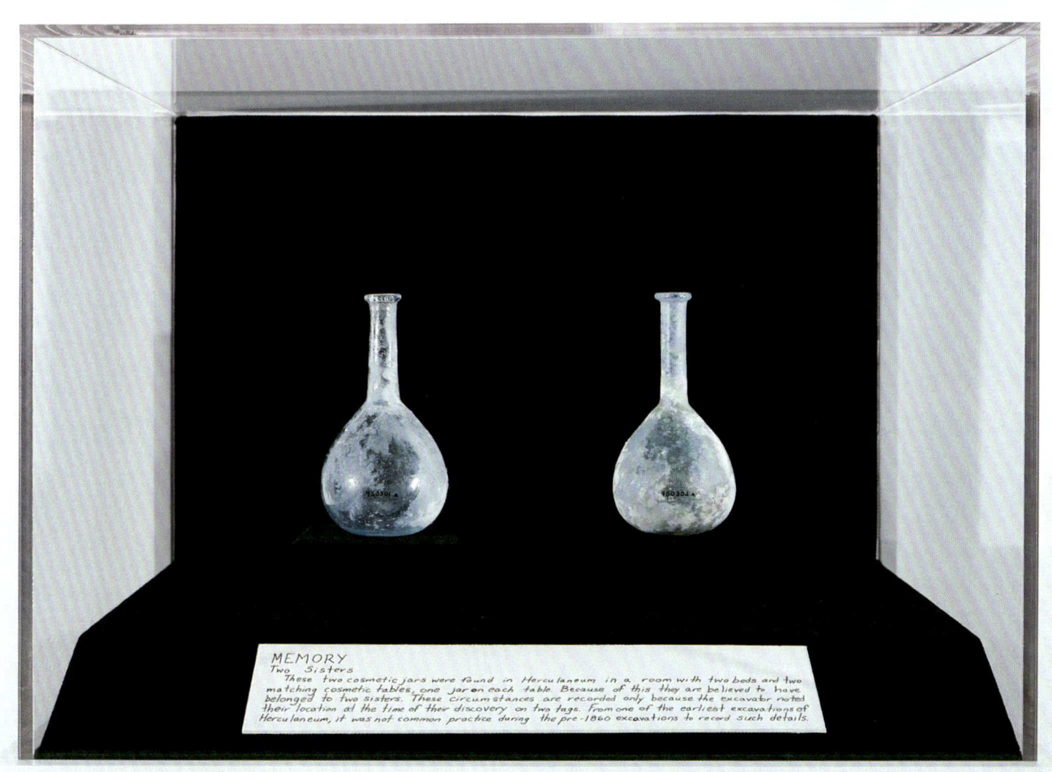

MEMORY
Two Sisters
These two cosmetic jars were found in Herculaneum in a room with two beds and two matching cosmetic tables, one jar on each table. Because of this they are believed to have belonged to two sisters. These circumstances are recorded only because the excavator noted their location at the time of their discovery on two tags. From one of the earliest excavations of Herculaneum, it was not common practice during the pre-1860 excavations to record such details.

THE THEORY OF FIRE
Blown glass, text, display
29 x 36 x 11 inches
1995
Collection of Martin Zimmerman, Linc Group, Chicago

The following is a copy of the text from the work

The practical Roman glass shapes in this case were etched by the great fire from the eruption of Mt. Vesuvius in A.D. 79, when ash trapped and buried glass in the cities of Pompeii and Herculaneum. In the conflagration fire, smoke, and ash swirled in the air, attacking the surface of these rare and fragile survivors of the Pompeiian catastrophe. This gave the everyday glass a desirable iridescent and black aspect. These specimens, once nothing but plain glass are now reminiscent of mother of pearl and the wings of butterflies. Many people want to acquire their own piece of ancient glass, because it is beautiful, because of its history, and because each is visibly a survivor of the fire.

c. 1750

It has been known now for many decades that iridescence is caused by moisture in the burial environment. Most ancient glass is found in tombs, so it is impossible for all ancient glass to have come from Pompeii as the general public believed in the eighteenth century. Certain types and acidity of earth attack glass, leaving the material iridescent and weathered. Iridescence is an optical phenomenon called "interference" that occurs when the surface of a material refracts light, producing a beautiful shimmering effect. It is what makes the glass appealing for us, and is what is sought out by collectors. However, these collectors should also consider other aspects, such as form, in choosing works to acquire.

c. 1900

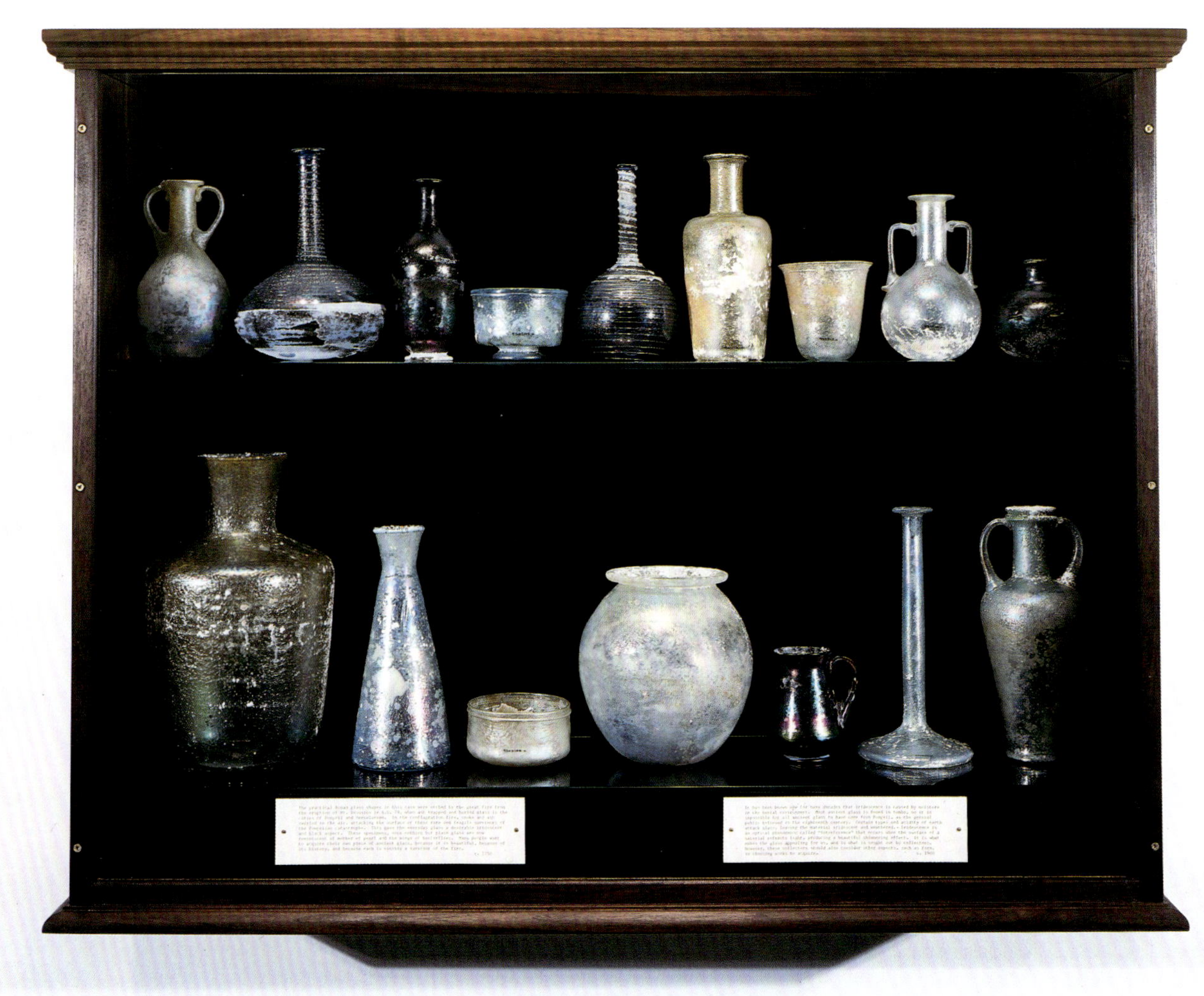

TRAVELS IN THE ROMAN EMPIRE (PLACES WHERE GLASS WAS MADE AND FOUND)
Blown glass, text, display
33 x 61 x 37 inches
1995
Courtesy of Donald Young Gallery, Chicago, Illinois

The following is a copy of the text from the work

Travels in the Roman Empire

   Deliberate copying of ancient glass has occurred since the beginning of this century . . . . . unlike the originals, ancient glass reproductions are frequently complete . . . . . a visit to a specialist museum will reveal just how little complete material has survived.

—Sotheby's

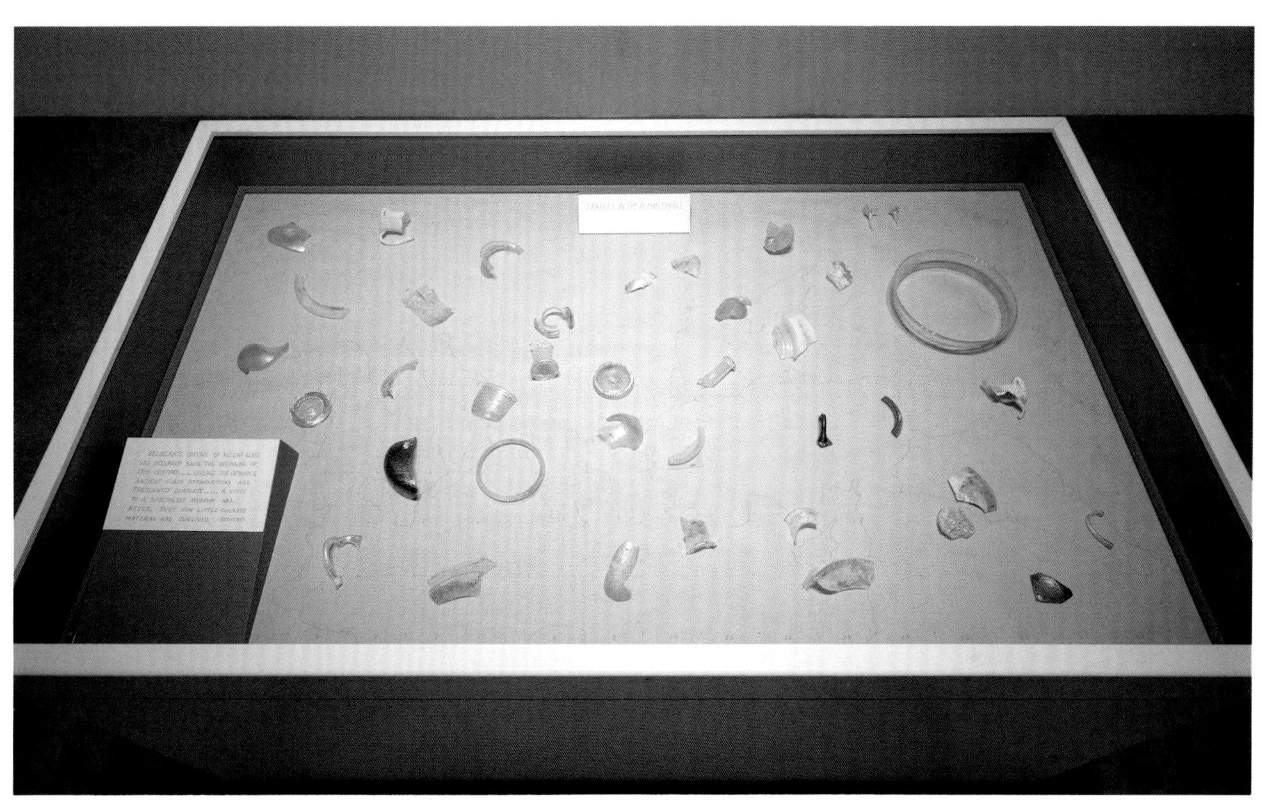

THE ONLY KNOWN GRAVE OF A GLASSBLOWER
Blown glass, text, display
48 x 72 x 36 inches
1994
Collection of the Seattle Art Museum, Seattle, Washington

The following is a selection of the text from the work

The Only Known Grave of a Glassblower:
Roman Glass found in Julius Alexander's tomb, 3rd century A.D.

From the invention of glassblowing until the Renaissance in Italy there is only one known grave of a glassblower. Other glassblowers' names are known through their signature imprint on mold blown objects, but only with a Roman glassblower Julius Alexander (alive in the third century) has a marked grave been found. He died and was buried near Lyons (in Gaul), and the grave stèle (stone), along with the glass found in his tomb, tells us something of his life.

Much of the ancient glass found today is recovered from tombs that protected it from the nearly inevitable breakage aboveground. The ancients buried domestic objects with their dead for use in the afterlife, and as a reminder of their former life.

We know that Julius Alexander was married, as his wife left the hairpin he made for her in his tomb (see label). We know that he practiced his art in Gaul but was a citizen of Rome, possibly born in Africa, Egypt, or Carthage.

We believe he blew the pieces found in the tomb but since they are without signature we can only be sure that he made the hairpin. Earlier historians attribute certain bottles found in Rome to his workshop. The stèle is in the Musèe des Beaux Arts at Lyons. In his tomb was common domestic glass of the third century, six bottles, four plates, two cups, one hairpin.

HAIRPIN
3rd century
Blue-green, intact glass, blown
Made by Julius Alexander for his wife. As he died before her, she placed it in his tomb as a memorial.
9403102.d

CUP
3rd century
Blue-green, intact glass with blown foot folded out of body
9403101.d

BOTTLE
3rd century
Blue-green, intact glass with blown, folded lip
The interior of the bottle is free of residue.
9403110.d

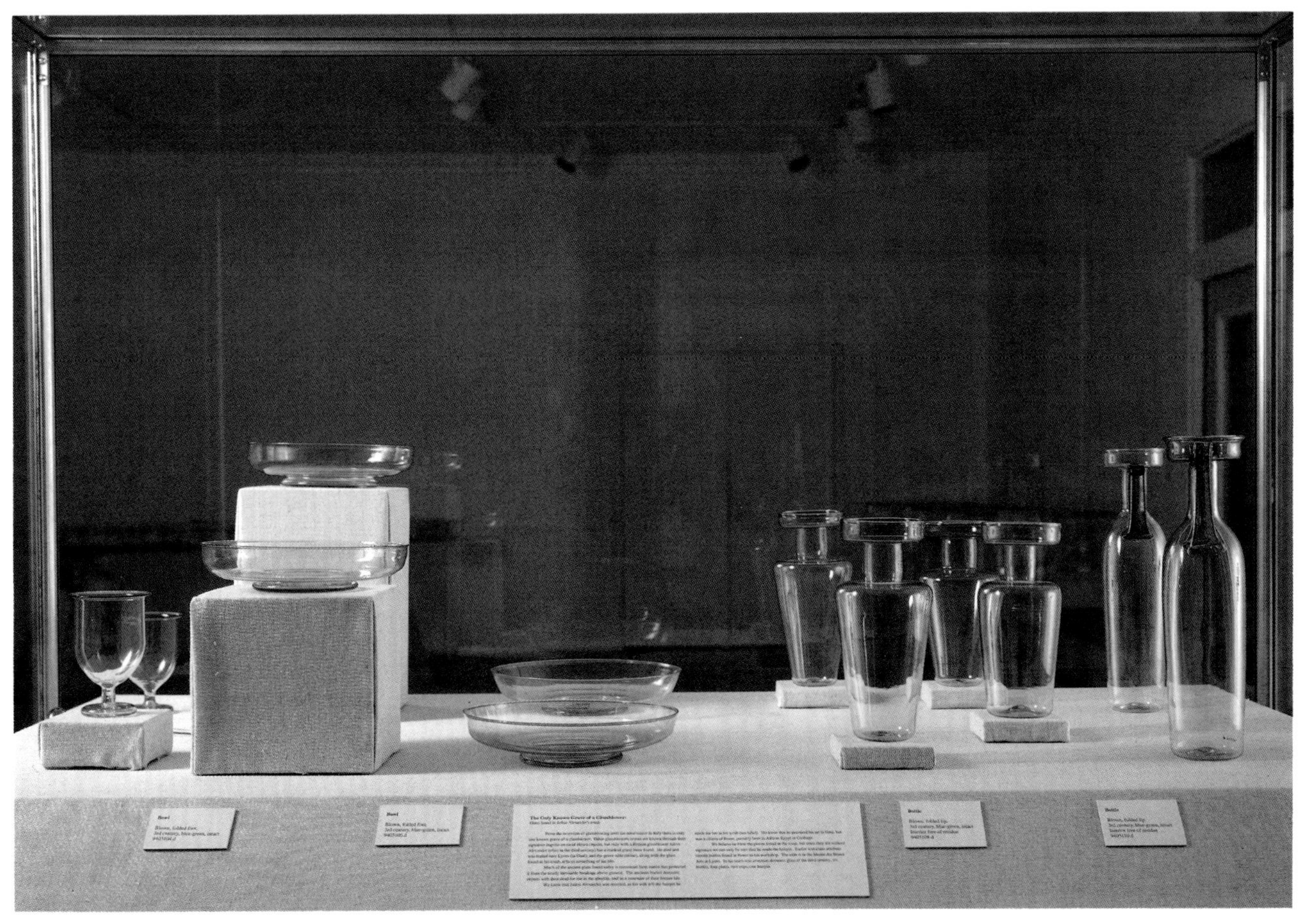

THE HISTORY OF SWEDISH GLASS BRIDAL CROWNS
Blown, engraved glass, text, display
24 x 51 x 17 inches
1993
Collection of Victoria Milne

The following is a copy of the text from the work

The History of Swedish Glass Bridal Crowns

At a Swedish wedding, the bride wears a crown instead of a veil during the ceremony; it is typically made of metal. In some areas, the mother of the bride will grow a myrtle bush and weave her daughter a crown or decorate a metal crown with its branches. The glass bridal crown is only known in the southern area of Sweden called Småland, which is the center for glass manufacturing.

Symbols
Engraved on each crown are the leaves and flowers of the myrtle of Sweden (myrtus communis v. tarentino). Traditionally, myrtus communis represents fertility and life. In Isaiah 41:19 "Isaiah, restoring dry barren desert and wilderness with life-giving trees, declares: 'I will plant in the wilderness the cedar, the shittah tree and the myrtle and the oil tree; I will set in the desert the fir tree and the pine, and the box tree together.' " Engraved on the first and second crown is the leaf of the alpine burl or European white birch. This common tree's beautiful heart-shaped leaves were used to decorate homes and gathering halls during the midsummer fertility celebration.

Use
Bridal crowns are kept at the church and can be used by many brides over the centuries. They are part of elaborate hair preparations, and are tied into the hair with pins and bands crisscrossing the bottom of the crowns. The process of securing them to the bride's head may take a full day. Glass crowns were often made by a glass master at the factory for his own daughters. Queen Kristina's monogrammed crown was never used. Kristina was the first queen of Sweden, ascending to the throne at a young age, and remembered for her forthrightness and the political changes made during her reign.

THE FIRST GLASS BRIDAL CROWN	THE SECOND GLASS BRIDAL CROWN	QUEEN KRISTINA'S BRIDAL CROWN
Blown glass, engraved	Blown glass, engraved	Blown glass, engraved
Date unknown—16th century ?	Date unknown—17th century ?	17th or 18th century
Possibly made at earliest factory at Trästenshult, Småland (the oldest glass factory in Sweden)	Possibly made at later Trästenshult factory	Possibly made by Italian immigrants at Kungsholm factory, Stockholm
930401.d	930403.d	930402.d

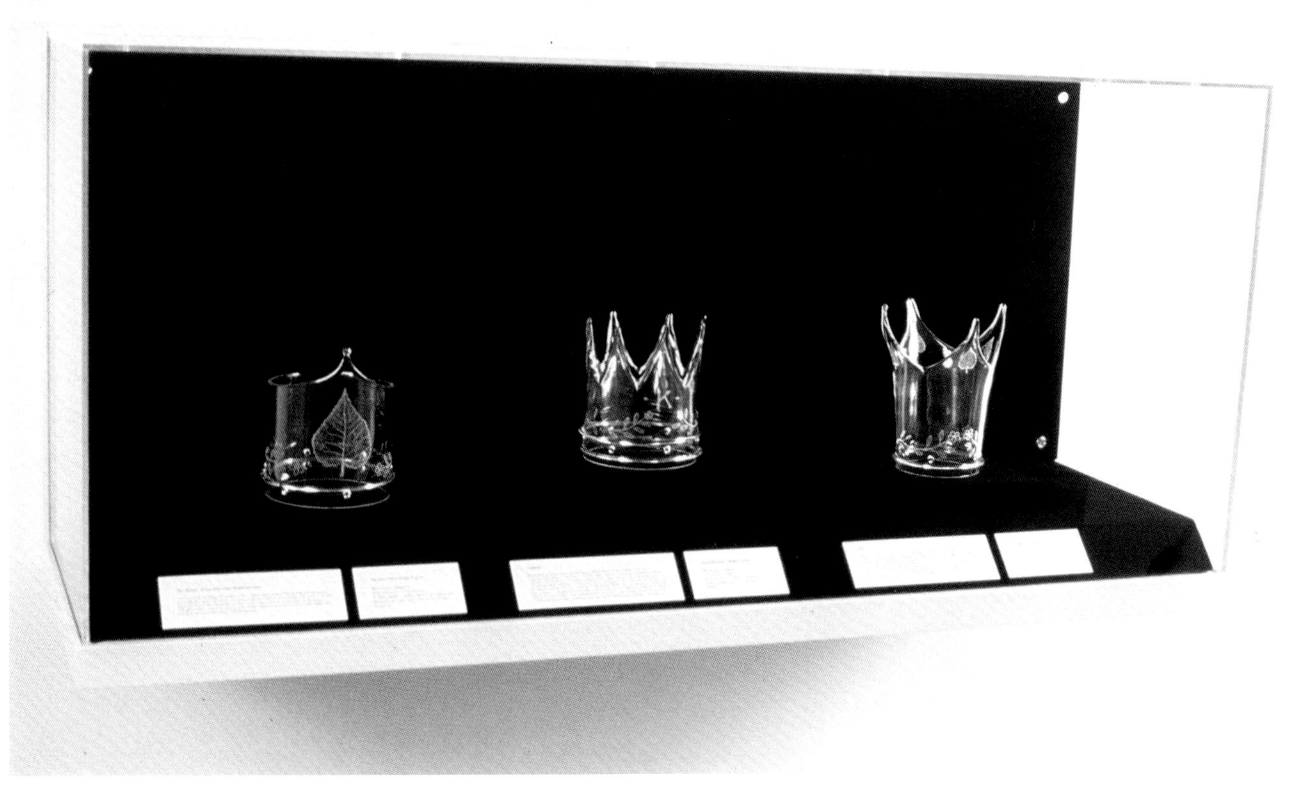

PLEDGE: THE FIRST GLASS LOVING CUPS
Blown, engraved, and flameworked glass, certificate, made on commission for couples only
8 x 8 inches
1994
Courtesy the Artist, AC Project Room, New York, New York; and Donald Young Gallery, Chicago, Illinois

The following is a copy of the text from the certificate that accompanies the work

The First Glass Loving Cups (replica)

This set of linked goblets was made by a late 16th or early 17th-century glassblower on the island of Murano, Venice. He made them during his lunch hour to celebrate a wedding in his own family. The links are made out of glass to remind one of the delicacy of relationships and the care which must be taken with them. The two offset rings in the stem represent the wedding bands and the endlessly intertwining white canes within them symbolize the permanence of union. The First Glass Loving Cups are well known on Murano for the fine lampworked joinery of the chain, and therefore the poignant delicacy with which they must be used. Two people can drink from them at the same time only if they hold the cups in a certain manner. The goblets may have been used in a wedding ceremony or privately by the couple.

A loving cup is a traditional vessel in metal, ceramic or glass used to celebrate a wedding or marriage. It can be a large communal cup or a pair of cups used in the wedding ceremony, shared either by the couple only or by all those present. Loving cups were also made as commemorations, decorated with portraits of the couple, the date of the wedding, a pair of joined initials, or depictions of allegorical wedding scenes. While individually similar to other Venetian empire goblets, the glass chain that permanently connects this pair is unique in the history of loving cups.

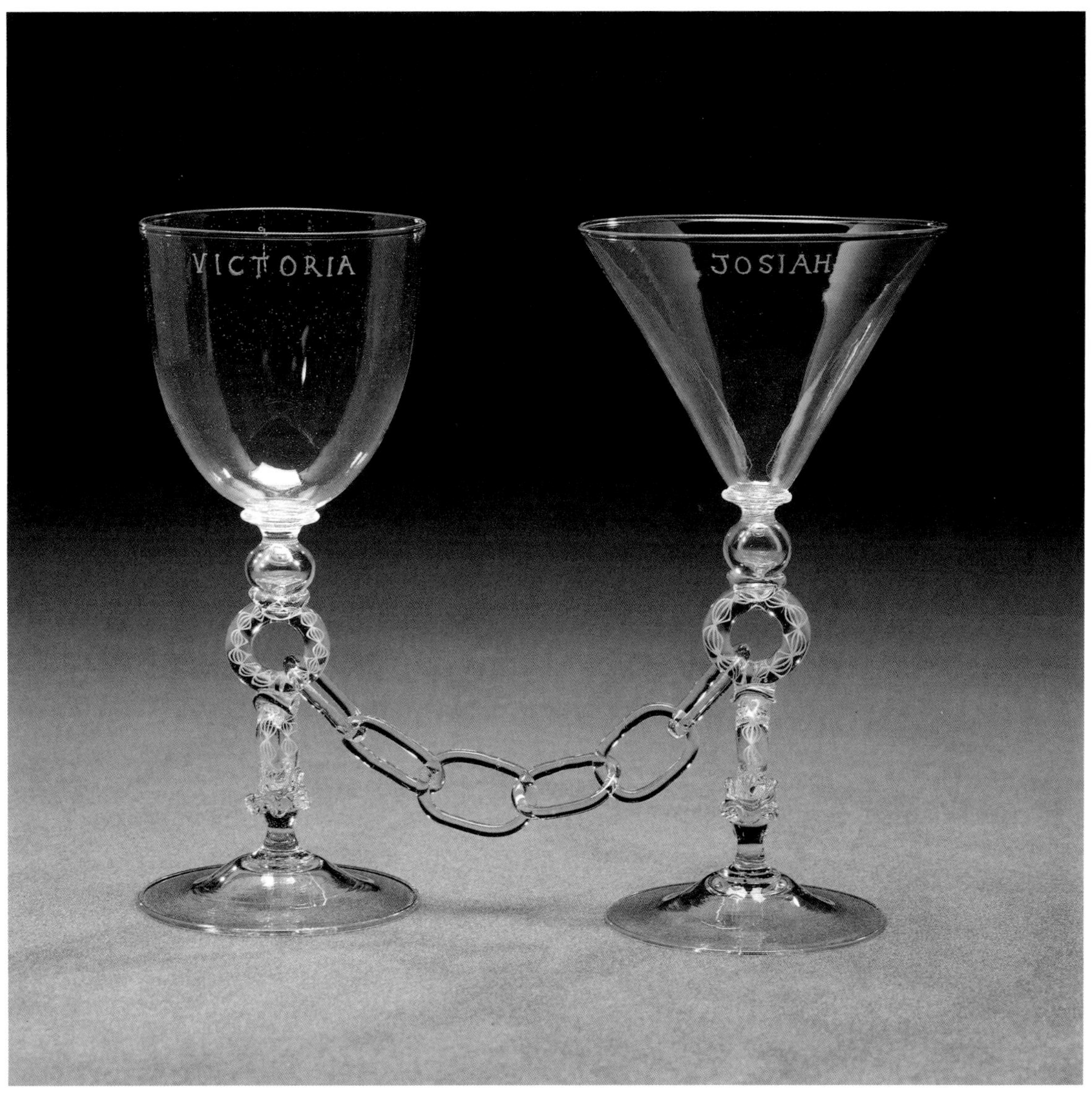

VICTORIA
JOSIAH

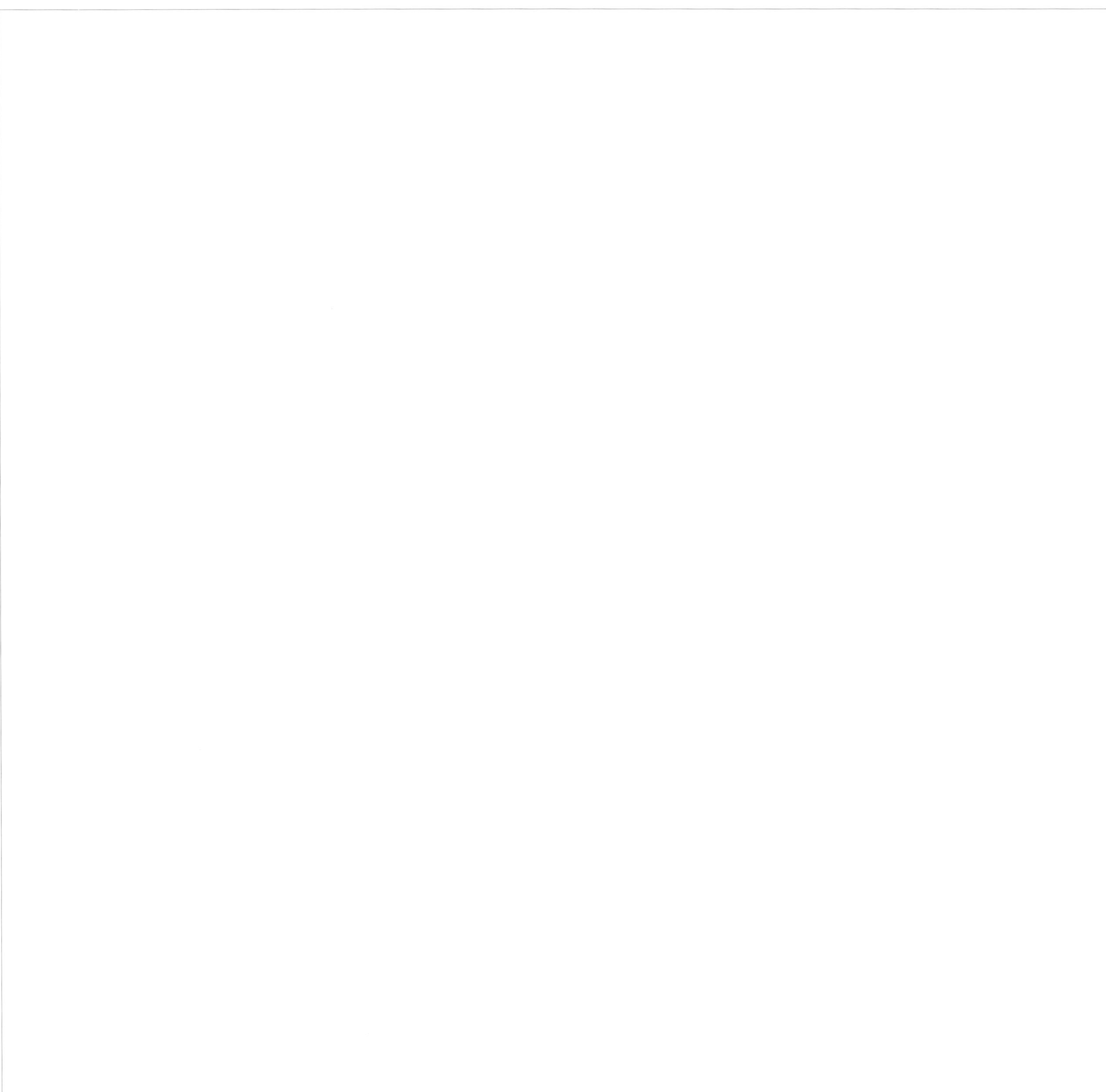

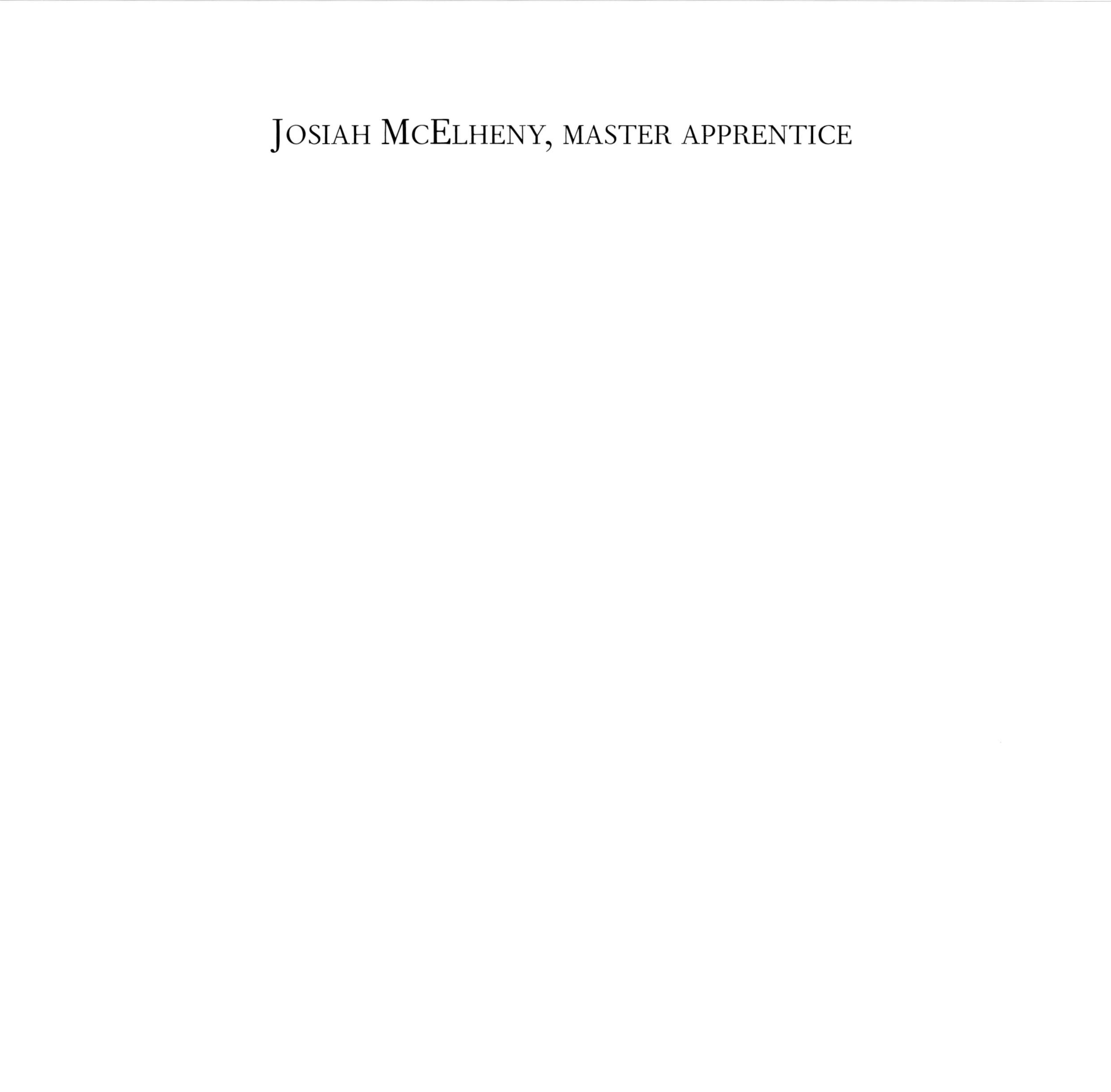
JOSIAH MCELHENY, MASTER APPRENTICE

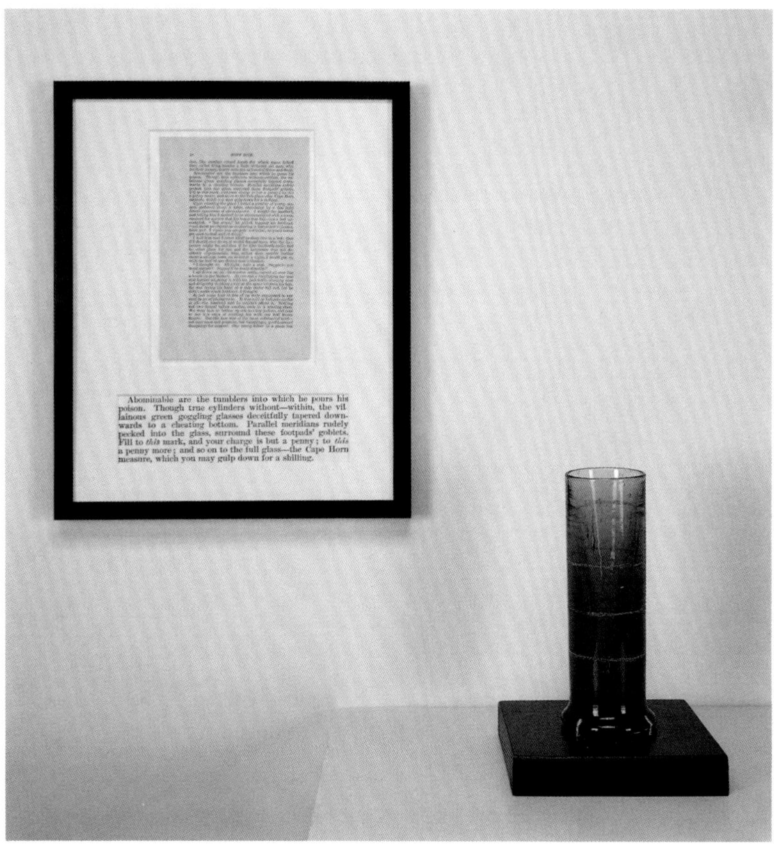

The Abominable Tumbler; blown glass, display, page from *Moby Dick*, text; framed text 12 x 14 inches, object 6 x 6 x 10 inches; 1998

Courtesy the Artist, AC Project Room, New York, New York; and Donald Young Gallery, Chicago, Illinois

Josiah McElheny, master apprentice

In 1918, while on a brief visit to Paris, Marcel Duchamp engaged a pharmacist to empty a glass ampule of serum and reseal it, filling it with 50cc of Parisian air, the perfect gift for his good friend in New York, Walter Arensberg. While Arensberg—who by this time already had assembled one of the most extensive collections of modern French art in the world—was a person with few worldly needs, Duchamp thought he lacked an essential elixir for wholeness as a cultural connoisseur, a breath of Parisian air. Duchamp inscribed Arensberg's dosage, "Sérum Physiologique," definitively identifying it as the unseeable, immaterial cure for Arensberg's affliction of a limiting human condition.

This transparent glass container came to Arensberg as a kind of surety for the logic of *Large Glass*, a work that consumed Duchamp's interest for almost a decade and that eventually came to reside with the Arensberg Collection. This readymade of 50cc of Parisian air was created on the heels of Duchamp's completion of a portion of *Large Glass* that he had given to another of his patrons, Katherine Drier. *To Be Looked At (From the Other Side of the Glass) with One Eye, Close To, for Almost an Hour* was one of a number of works from this period that were executed on the surface of glass, a plane unfettered by optical finality or illusionistic resolution, and which confirmed the perpetual "makingness" inherent in optical experience. As a study for *Large Glass*, this work with its elaborate viewing directives focused on the core concern in Duchamp's address of modernism, that art was not an opaque plane of information but a transparent field of intellectual and experiential opportunity. In order to see art clearly, one needed to perpetually reassess one's position in relation to it, to come at it from all sides.

"Sérum Physiologique," unfettered by form, was a cure for what ailed modern art and its perception as form over and above its life as idea. Duchamp's 50cc of life's essential vapor were suspended in a glass container as idea. While comprehensible as finite material, this breath of Paris was unquantifiable, more allegory than reality. Irrefutably familiar as the substance that sustained all life, it was wholly elusive as matter. Duchamp had presented Arensberg with a sample of an idea whose mass was no more or less real than its unnamed chemical counterpart outside the transparent container. It was art on faith, as natural or unconscious a belief to Duchamp as breathing. The work's glass ampule, drafted from its intended purpose as a bearer of liquid into a bearer of meaning, subtly set understanding off from the traditional expectations that eagerly pressed in around it anxiously hoping to convert it back into ordinary oxygen.

The glass elements in Josiah McElheny's installations are not conscripted away from customary uses but from their traditional cultural perception as objects, into the service of art and beauty. This is particularly clear in *Studies in the Search for Infinity* and *Verzelini's Acts of Faith*, in which he attempts to persuade the viewer that these works were not undertaken as explorations of form but of certain ideals. His work is not a depiction of modernity or history, it is an embodiment of ideas as the given form of art. Utilizing the power behind the centuries-old craft of glassblowing, rather than the sputtering engine of postmodernist intellectual sleights of meaning, McElheny makes his thinking perfectly transparent, forming it into objects that he presents just out of reach of any definitive contextualizing narrative or functional purpose. Unlike Duchamp's ampule, McElheny's glass develops and satisfies one's taste for material beauty and well-crafted ideas. Yet, like the master Duchamp in his defiance of modernist values, McElheny makes one uneasy in the admiration of this beauty formed by logic.

McElheny's Socratic apprenticeship to modernism is not apparent on one's initial encounter with his installations. His glassworks appear as historical records, physical documents of bygone cultures and master craftsmen. On closer inspection of the objects and their contextualizing narratives, it becomes clear that there is a dysfunction between the viewer's actual encounter with the work and its "explanation": that, in fact, this must be the work of a contemporary artist, as the narratives do not tell one the content of the installation but are intended to make the viewer's expectation of narrative as the subject matter of art obsolete. Ironically, the texts accomplish this through their placement of the viewer within an experience of art yet outside the histories of both craft and idea as the "answer" to this experience. These are unusable vessels and unreliable ideas. Would one dare eat off a plate crafted in the pursuit of infinity or drink from a miraculous cup? Yet one would also not be comfortable with the consideration of these works as merely exquisite conceptual pranks. McElheny's practice is enigmatic to glassmakers, who are indifferent to his conceptual concern for history and fiction in his apprenticeship to modernism, and to conceptual artists, who would readily scoff at the value conveyed in McElheny's devotion to the craft tradition of glassblowing and the disciplines and self-abnegation inherent in its apprentice system. Equalizing the transparency of meaning in the traditions of glassblowing and art history, McElheny defies the limits of both schools as he translates the beauty in practice and ideas into a cohesive corpus of specific objects.

McElheny mediates the disparity between the relative abilities of matter and word to yield meaning. In *The Abominable Tumbler* this is conveyed as he interprets Melville's words in their artful crafting of unsightly forms by creating the object described in the novel *Moby Dick*. McElheny gives form to the imagined vessels through which Melville endeavored to yield an allegory of the dissolution of human hope: "Abominable are the tumblers into which he pours his poison. Though true cylinders without—within, the villainous green goggling glasses deceitfully tapered downwards to a cheating bottom. Parallel meridians rudely pecked into the glass, surround these footpads' goblets. Fill to *this* mark, and your charge is but a penny; to *this* a penny more; and so on to the full glass— the Cape Horn measure, which you may gulp down for a shilling." In his literalizing of this glass, McElheny undermines imagination for the sake of clarity, to embody the allegory inherent in language and reveal the common goal of word and object to yield experience. This charge to art transcends the histories of both mediums.

In his devotion to the traditional craft of glassblowing and its complex, yet clear, bond to a history of signi-fied meanings, McElheny echoes Duchamp's own apprenticeship to modernism, a tradition that wed idea and action, as laid out by its first theoretician Charles Baudelaire in *The Painter of Modern Life* in 1863. In this text, Baudelaire urged the artists of his day to unite the "ephemeral, the fugitive, the contingent" of their modern expe-rience with the "eternal and the enduring" of their inherited traditions. The source of Baudelaire's urging was his desire to save art from the ill fate of both academicism and rote illustration, the forms so excessively parodied by artists practicing in a "post-modernist" vein today. For Duchamp, the practice of modernism led to the fore-grounding of idea as the essential form of art, while for McElheny, adherence to this faith results in an art that is in contradiction to recent popular modernist practice, his creation of beauty with formal and conceptual intent. For McElheny, the tradition of modernism hinges on the legacy of knowledge as experience. In his work it depends, as once identified by the sculptor Donald Judd in his watershed essay "Specific Objects"—in which he analyzed the practice of Minimalist artists in the 1960s as reactionary to the traditions of modernism—on the viewer's knowledge of real objects.

In the practice of modernism, materials define the parameters of artistic inquiry. In order to find out about painting, sculpting, glassblowing, one must respond to paint, canvas, wood, and glass. For Minimalist artists working in the 1960s, such as Judd, Andre, Morris, and Serra, the motivation to follow this course of inquiry was supplemented by a desire to relieve the process of making form in the twentieth century from its anticipated ser-vice of subjective expression. They wanted to show that meaning was on the outside of objects, not hidden in tradition or in transposed, metaphorical readings. For these artists and McElheny, meaning has been achieved through the wedding of words and materials through actions in time and in space. As Rosalind Krauss wrote in her essay on Minimalism, "The Double Negative: A New Syntax for Sculpture," in 1977, "Minimalist sculptors began with a procedure for declaring the externality of meaning," and they did this by abandoning themselves to the creation of form by creating simple equations using industrial materials such as steel, lead, and brick and artless transitive verbs:

> to roll
>
> to crease
>
> to fold
>
> to store
>
> to bend
>
> to shorten
>
> to twist
>
> to twine
>
> to cut
>
> to stack . . .

As they laid out prefabricated industrial material according to select ritualized actions, these sculptors, like McElheny with his transparent glass, created art without the limiting surface of painting or the unknowable inte-rior of sculpture, art that was neither abstract nor figurative. What distinguishes McElheny's practice from that of these Minimalists is that the art tradition to which he has apprenticed himself is not bounded by the limiting conditions of material but by the limiting conditions of art history and its ideas of art. In the tradition of Duchamp, McElheny is not attempting to free his work from the prescribed forms of his medium nor his subjective manipulation of its terms but of the traditions that determine the limits of the broader context of art experience.

It is in his submission to the collective history of glassblowing that McElheny is released from the fetters of modernism, the limits of material and subjective expression. McElheny creates his art through mystifying ritualistic actions that are not his own; they belong to the tradition of glassblowing and rely on the joint effort of a group of artisans. These procedures are undertaken by a team of initiates who assist McElheny in a craft with no written canon, handed down through generations of master glassblowers. Their art has been learned by gesture, their work often the product of wordless communication.

Curiously, this practice does possess its own list of transitive verbs, an unrecorded language developed to name actions determined by the material's own history:

marvering

gathering

blocking

jacking

puntying

knocking

tweezing

flashing

paddling

cracking off . . .

Unlike the Minimalists' accessible, yet impersonal, subjection of industrial materials to common actions, McElheny's handmade transparent objects are the result of an operation that is less subjective and yet is indecipherable to outsiders because it is so firmly rooted in a verbal tradition. The term "marvering" provides a particularly good example of how process in glassmaking moved language through action in order to identify meaning. This verb describes the action of rolling molten glass on a table. It is believed that the origin of the word comes from the place, a marble table, on which the rolling occurred, thereby yielding the word marbling. Through the centuries marbling became marveling, the named response in the observer to the effect of such an action. Eventually this marveling was transformed from the observer back to the observed, to the action of marvering, the place in time in glassblowing where the marvel came into being in the creation of a specific object.

The artist's presentations of series of glass elements created in the pursuit of a particular idea, as in *History of Mirrors* or *The Development of Social Critique*, are efforts to draw or diagram ideas through process. His looking glasses are real illusions. When the works in these series are presented as a whole, they represent the specific object as it exists as an ideal, beyond and between the physical forms that are actually made manifest in the world. Using drawing, photographs, text, and titling, McElheny clarifies what would otherwise remain opaque, that the relationship between the two-dimensional realm of ideas and three-dimensional life of objects is the essence of the endeavor. Unlike the efforts of his conceptualist predecessors, McElheny has the advantage of the ideal medium for his efforts; glass literally embodies what the artist Ree Morton defined as the space in art-making that combined the real, the imaginary, and the illusionary, "air plus object." Its transparency reiterates that meaning is not to be found on its surface, that it hovers in, beyond, and through the material that has drawn an ideal into the world.

McElheny's apprenticeship to modernism and its theoretical progeny is the motive behind his apprenticeship to the traditions of glassblowing. Brought to the medium for its rich legacy of transmitting experience into form, McElheny became an initiate in the glassblower's faith. The expansive nature of this experience encouraged him to further his practice as an artist through his study under other traditions in the humanities that inform and bound the life of art and from which he draws inspiration: painting, sculpture, literature, mythology, religion, archaeology, philosophy, etc. What is unique about McElheny's achievement as a recent practitioner within the tradition of modernism is how his specific objects make their conceptual, textual counterparts obsolete. The texts are only as necessary as maps are to those who are lost. As soon as viewers find their way back to McElheny's objects, they may be summarily disregarded. His adherence to the thinking histories of sculptors, painters, curators, collectors, conservators, and philosophers leads him back to the practice of glassblowing. In fact, if the texts for his works were compiled, they would read as a manual that explicates the possible motives and disciplines for a modern apprenticeship in the tradition of glassblowing: to find one's place in history, to free form from ornamentation, to understand specific objects, to celebrate materials, to critique cultural tradition, and to honor one's faith.

It is in the review of such a manual that Josiah McElheny's vision as an artist would find resonance with Isabella Stewart Gardner's practice as a museum maker. Both their endeavors were undertaken in order to make art seen beyond the limiting terms determined by the physical boundaries of the human condition and tradition. The cultural inquiry outlined in McElheny's manual applies to Isabella Gardner's own unique presentation of the specific objects she selected for her Museum, a practice between disciplines that has yet to be definitively named:

       philanthropy
       collecting
       curating
       art making
       cultural theorizing . . .

Perhaps the word marvering would do?

Jennifer R. Gross, Curator of Contemporary Art and Public Programs

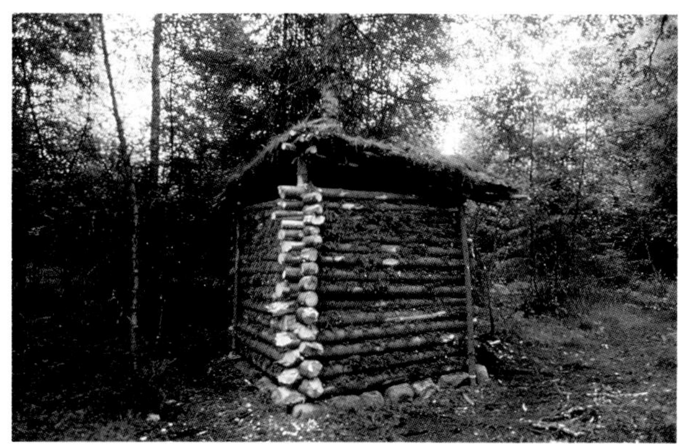

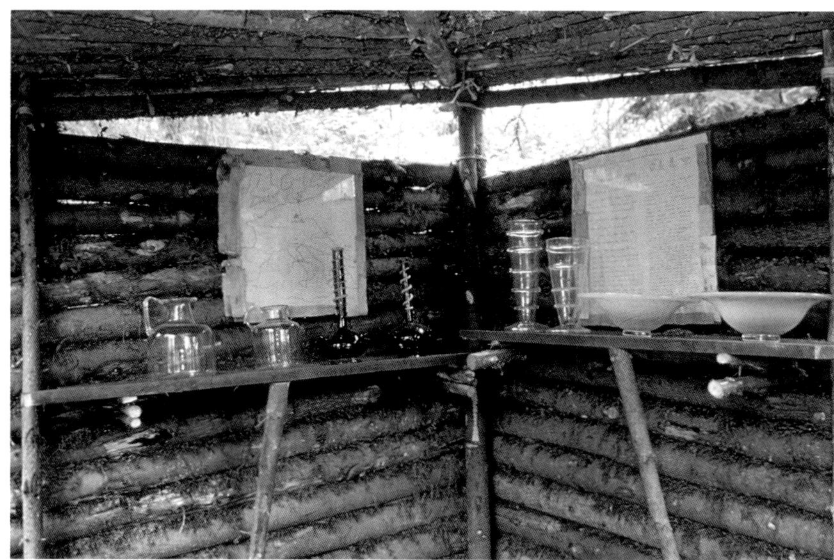

Jägarens Glasmuseet (The Hunter's Glass Museum); glass, display, text,
and drawing; 96 x 96 x 144 inches; 1990

Permanent installation in southern Sweden

Josiah McElheny: Biographical Information

1966   Born in Boston, Massachusetts

Education

1992–97   Apprentice to master glassblower Lino Tagliapietra; various locations
1989–91   Apprentice to master glassblowers Jan-Erik Ritzman and Sven-Åke Carlsson, Transjö, Sweden
1988   B.F.A., Rhode Island School of Design, Providence, Rhode Island
1987   European Honors Program, Rhode Island School of Design, Rome, Italy
            Studied with master glassblower Ronald Wilkinson, London, England

One-Person Exhibitions

1999   Henry Art Gallery, University of Washington, Seattle, Washington
            Isabella Stewart Gardner Museum, Boston, Massachusetts
1997   "Non-Decorative Beautiful Objects," AC Project Room, New York, New York
            "Three Alter Egos," Donald Young Gallery, Seattle, Washington
1996   Barbara Krakow Gallery, Boston, Massachusetts
1995   Donald Young Gallery, Seattle, Washington
            Stephen Friedman Gallery, London, England
            Installation in the Ancient Mediterranean and Egypt Gallery, Seattle Art Museum, Seattle, Washington
1994   "Authentic History," The Robert Lehman Gallery of the New York Experimental Glass Workshop, Brooklyn, New York
1993   "originals, fakes, reproductions," William Traver Gallery, Seattle, Washington
1990   "Jägarens Glasmuseet," (The Hunter's Glass Museum), permanent installation, Arnescruv, Sweden

Selected Group Exhibitions

1998   "Young Americans, Part II," The Saatchi Gallery, London, England
            "At Home in the Museum," Art Institute of Chicago, Illinois
            "Personal Touch," Art in General, New York, New York
            "Interlacings," Whitney Museum of Art at Hartford, Connecticut
            "Inglenook," Feigen Contemporary, New York, New York; and Illinois State University, Normal
            "Usefool," Postmasters Gallery, New York, New York
1997   "Living Room," Barbara Westerman Gallery, Newport, Rhode Island
            "Paul Bloodgood, Paula Hayes, Josiah McElheny and Sandra Vallejos," AC Project Room, New York, New York
1996   "A Labor of Love," The New Museum of Contemporary Art, New York, New York
            "What's Love Got to Do with It?" Randolph Street Gallery, Chicago, Illinois
            "The Last Supper," Donald Young Gallery, Seattle, Washington
            "Drawings from the Mab Library," AC Project Room, New York, New York
1995   "For Victoria," (with Dan Peterman), Andrea Rosen Gallery, New York, New York
            "For Victoria" (with Dan Peterman), Grazer Kunstverein, Graz, Austria
            "VER-RÜCKT," Kulturstiftung Schloss Agathenburg, Agathenburg, Germany; traveled to Art Museum of Arolsen
            "Documents Northwest: Holding the Past: Historicism in Northwest Glass," Seattle Art Museum, Seattle, Washington
1994   "Wunderkammer," Rena Bransten Gallery, San Francisco, California
            "Are You Experienced?" Andrea Rosen Gallery, New York, New York

Selected Bibliography (listed chronologically)

Israel, Nico. "Josiah McElheny at AC Project Room." Review. *Artforum*, March 1998.
Volk, Gregory. "Josiah McElheny at AC Project Room." Review. *Art in America*, February 1998.
Scanlan, Joe. "Josiah McElheny, AC Project Room, New York." Review. *Frieze Magazine*, January 1998.
"Josiah McElheny 'Non-Decorative Beautiful Objects.'" Review. *The New Yorker*, November 3, 1997.
Saltz, Jerry. "Josiah McElheny 'Non-Decorative Beautiful Objects.'" Reviews. *Time Out NY*, October 30–November 6, 1997.
Smith, Roberta. "Josiah McElheny 'Non-Decorative Beautiful Objects.'" Art Guide, *The New York Times*, October 24, 1997.
Smith, Roberta. "Josiah McElheny 'Non-Decorative Beautiful Objects.'" Art in Review, *The New York Times*, October 17, 1997.
Pedersen, Victoria. "Reconstructing the Moon." Preview. *Paper*, October 1997.
Glowen, Ron. "Josiah McElheny at Donald Young Gallery." *Artweek*, Febuary 1997.
Hackett, Regina. "Josiah McElheny's Glasswork Dazzles at Donald Young Gallery." *Seattle Post-Intelligencer*, January 31, 1997.
Fredericksen, Eric. "The Glass Artist." *The Stranger*, December 26, 1996–January 1, 1997.
Updike, Robin. "Looking Through the Glass at Art History and Authority." *The Seattle Times*, December 26, 1996.
Tucker, Marcia. *A Labor of Love*. New York: The New Museum of Contemporary Art, 1996.
Spalding, Kelly. "Josiah McElheny." *artsMEDIA*, Summer 1996.
Sherman, Mary. "Artist Shatters Reality with Glass Replicas." *Boston Sunday Herald*, July 7, 1996.
Buttler, Joachim and Nasim Weiler. *VER-RÜCKT*. Agathenburg: Kultursiftung Schloss Agathenburg, 1996.
Updike, Robin. "Reflecting the Past." *The Seattle Times*, July 11, 1995.
Melrod, George. "Openings: Future History." *Art & Antiques*, May 1995.
Volk, Gregory. "Josiah McElheny and Dan Peterman." *ARTnews*, May 1995.
"Josiah McElheny and Dan Peterman." Review. *The New Yorker*, February 20 and 27, 1995.
Smith, Roberta. "Josiah McElheny and Dan Peterman." *The New York Times*, February 10, 1995.
"Are You Experienced?" Review. *The New Yorker*, April 4, 1994.
Avgikos, Jan. "Josiah McElheny: The Art of Authentic Forgery." *Glass*, Winter 1993.
Oldknow, Tina. "Josiah McElheny." *Glass*, Fall 1993.
Kangas, Matthew. "Exhibition Review from Seattle, WA." *Sculpture*, September/October 1993.

Awards

1998	Bagley Wright Fund Award, Seattle, Washington
1996	Artist Grant, Art Matters, Inc., New York, New York
1995	Award Winner, 1995 Biennial Competition of the Louis Comfort Tiffany Foundation, New York, New York
1993	Betty Bowen Special Recognition Award, Seattle Art Museum, Seattle, Washington

Selected Professional Experience

1997	Småland Museum, Sweden; co-curator with Ann Wolff of "Transjö i Världen" (Transjö in the World)
1996	Haystack School, Deer Isle, Maine; teaching assistant to Swedish glassmaster Jan-Erik Ritzman
1995	Pilchuck Glass School, Stanwood, Washington; teaching assistant for Italian glassmasters Lino Tagliapietra and Checco Ongero
1995	Rhode Island School of Design, Providence, Rhode Island; visiting faculty

Dave Hickey is a critic, musician, and professor of art criticism and theory at the University of Nevada, Las Vegas. He was owner-director of A Clean Well-Lighted Place in Austin, Texas, and director of Reese Palley Gallery in New York. He has served as executive editor for *Art in America* and as staff songwriter for Glaser Publications in Nashville, Tennessee. In 1989, he published *Prior Convictions*, a volume of short fiction.

His book *The Invisible Dragon: Four Essays on Beauty* (1992) brought the issues of "beauty" and "value" to the fore of art discussions in the nineties. In his most recent book, *Air Guitar* (1997), Hickey boldly addresses the issue of art as a form of currency, subject to rituals of commerce. In 1994, Dave Hickey received the Frank Jewett Mather Award for Distinction in Art Criticism, the highest award in the field.

Jennifer R. Gross is curator of contemporary art and public programs at the Isabella Stewart Gardner Museum in Boston. Gross came to the Gardner Museum from the Institute of Contemporary Art at the Maine College of Art in Portland, Maine, where she was director. During her tenure as director, Gross oversaw the design and construction of the ICA@MECA and curated exhibitions by such artists as Peter Campus, Maureen Connor, John Coplans, David Ireland, Matthew McCaslin, Beverly Semmes, and Jessica Stockholder. While at the Maine College of Art, Gross was assistant professor, lecturing in critical theory and contemporary art.

Gross obtained a B.A. degree from Lafayette College, Easton, Pennsylvania, in International Affairs; an M.A. in art history from Hunter College, New York, New York; and is currently a doctoral candidate at the City University of New York, Graduate Center. The subject of her dissertation is the American artist Richard Tuttle.